I0461881

Real World
Colouring Book
For Advanced Users & Adults

50 Images

Created From Real Life Photos For You To Colour As You Please.

ISBN 978-0-359-83323-8
90000
9 780359 833238

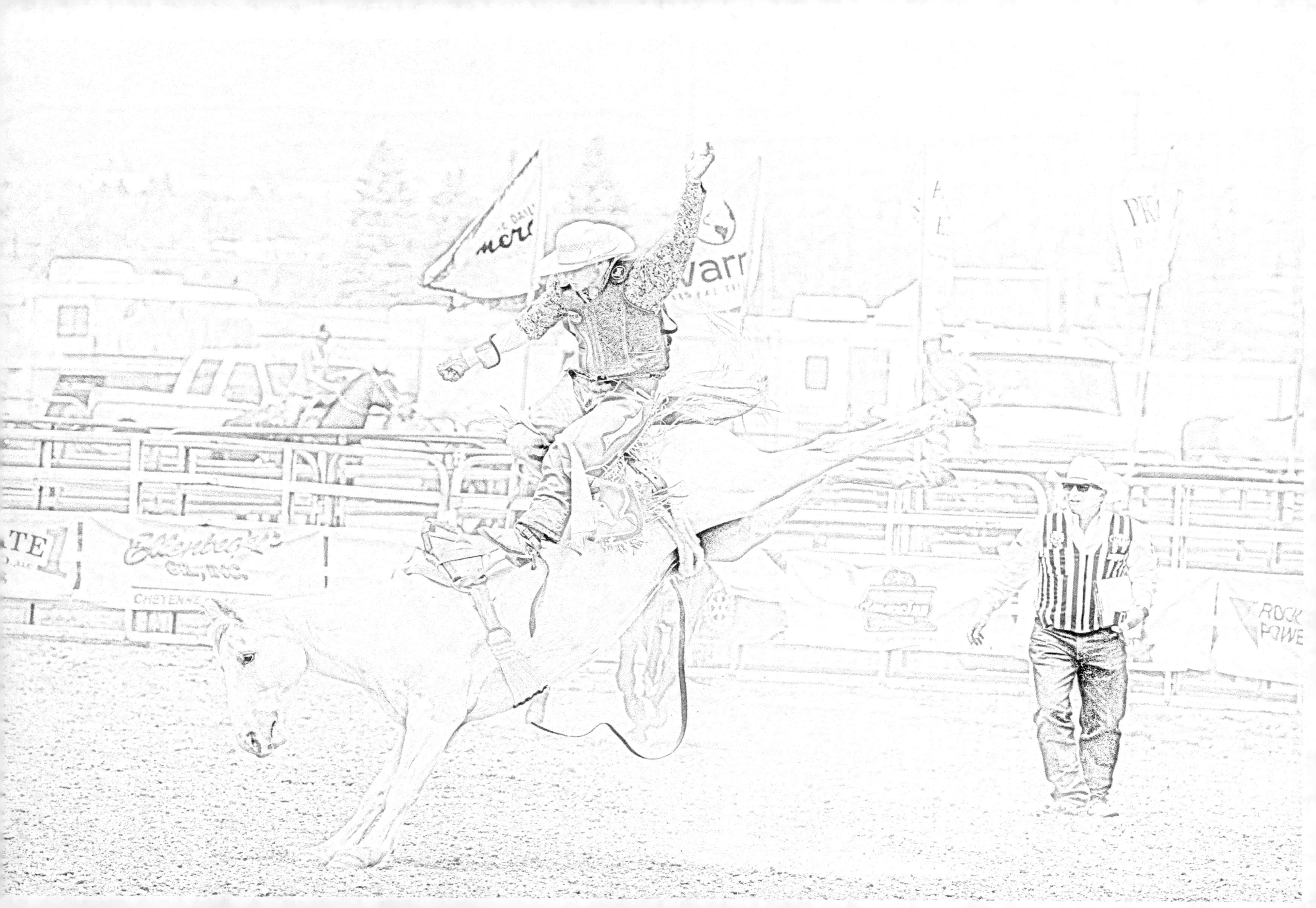

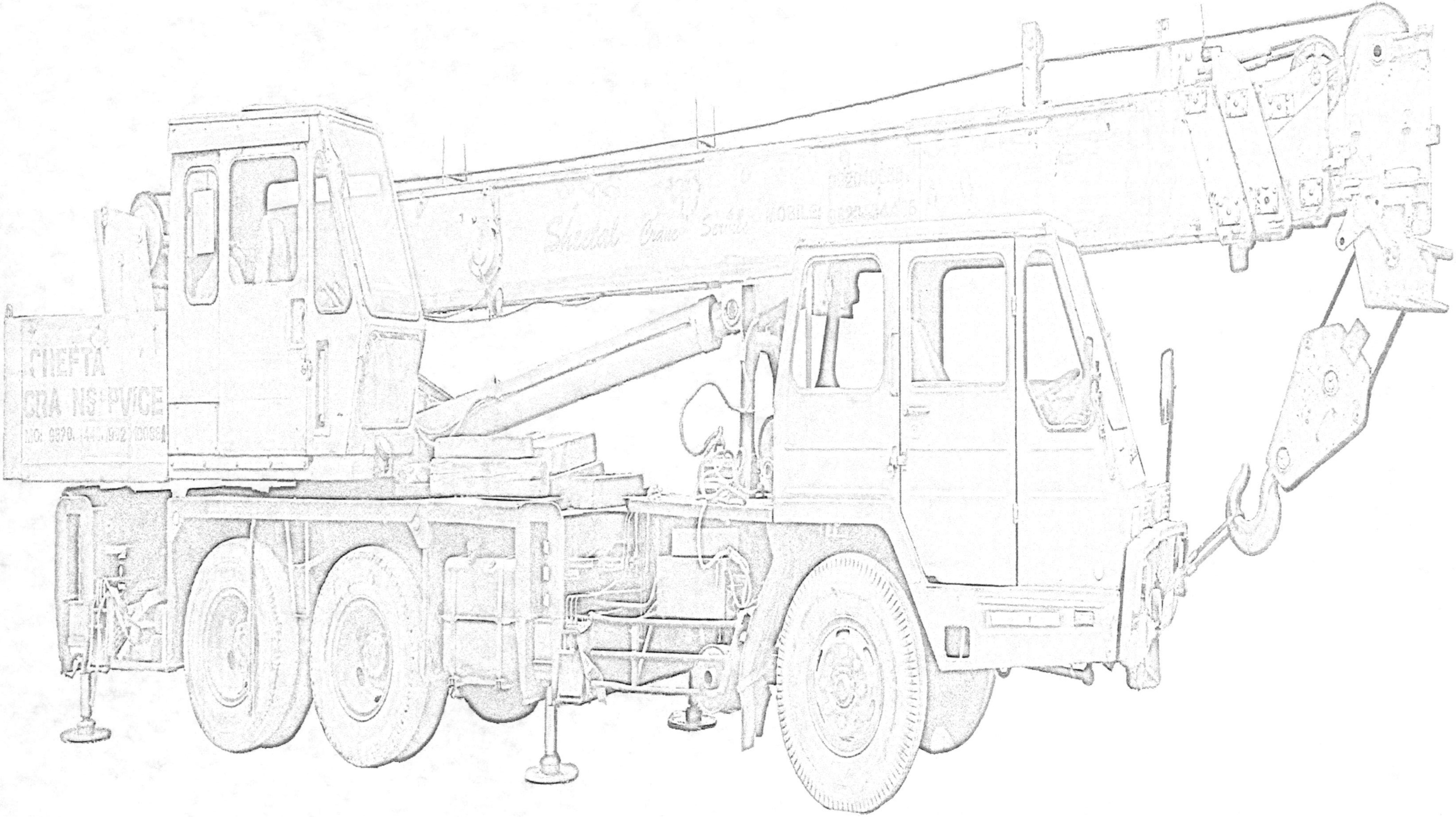

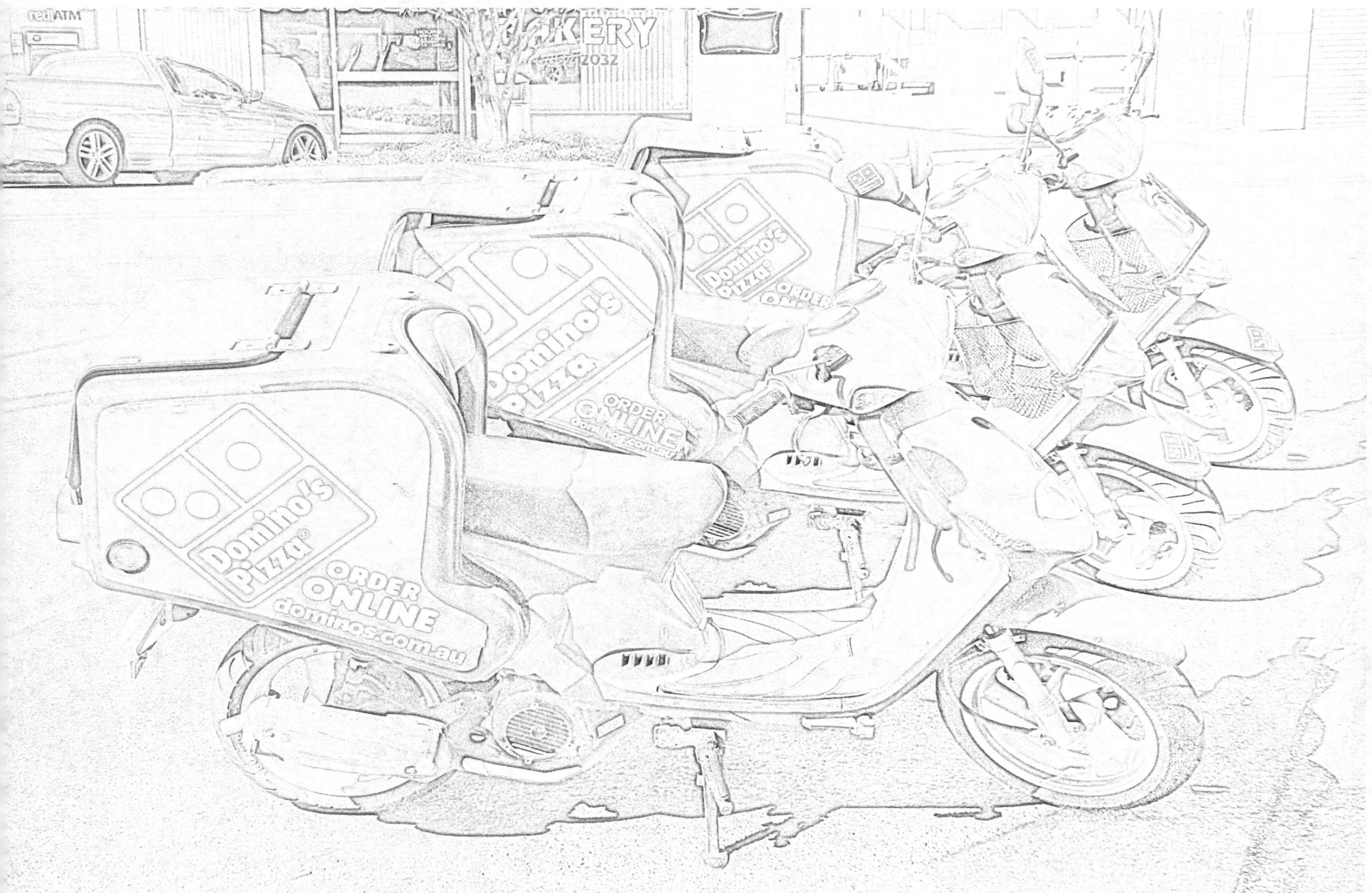
redATM
KERY
2032
Domino's Pizza
ORDER ONLINE
dominos.com.au
Domino's Pizza
ORDER ONLINE
Domino's Pizza
ORDER

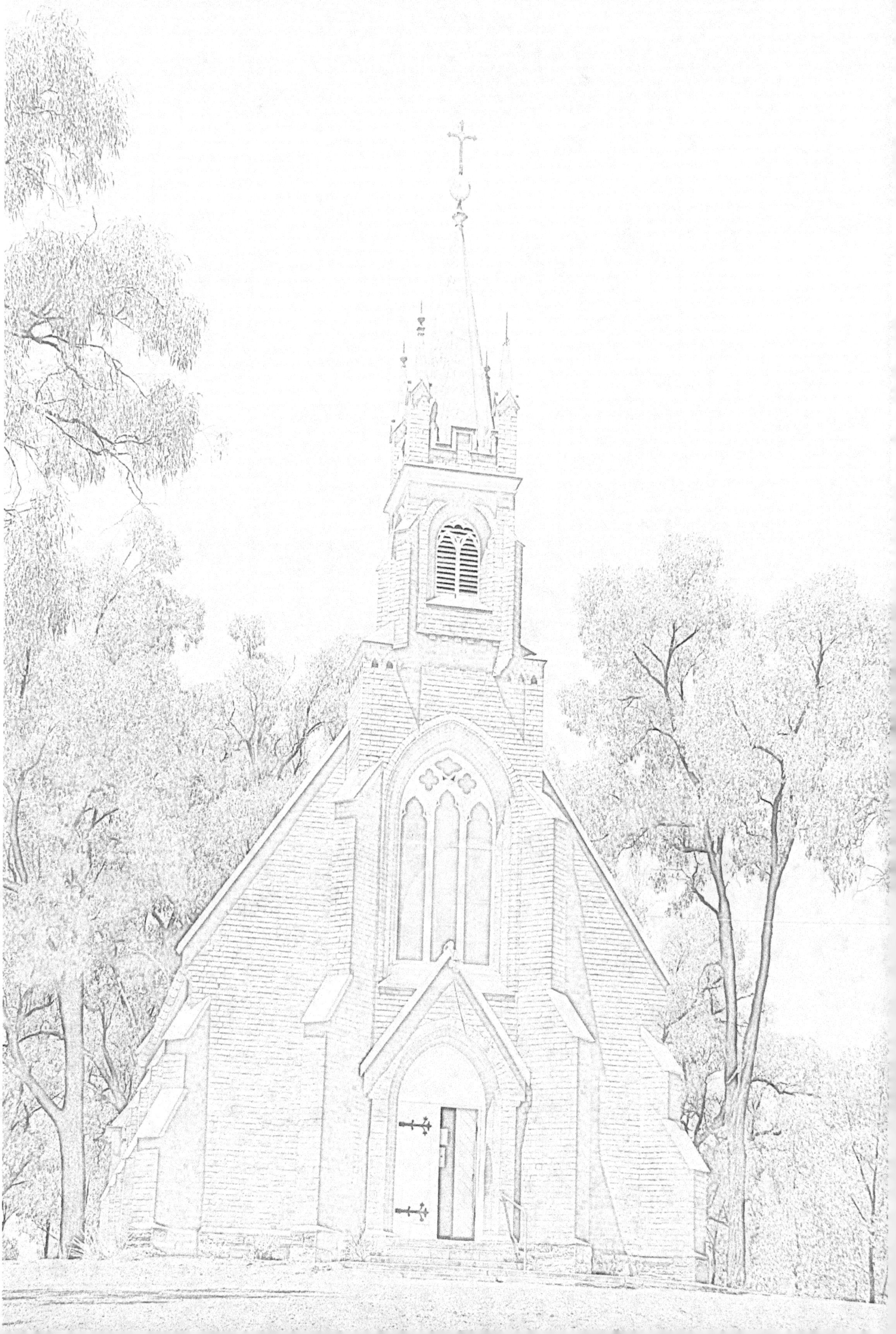

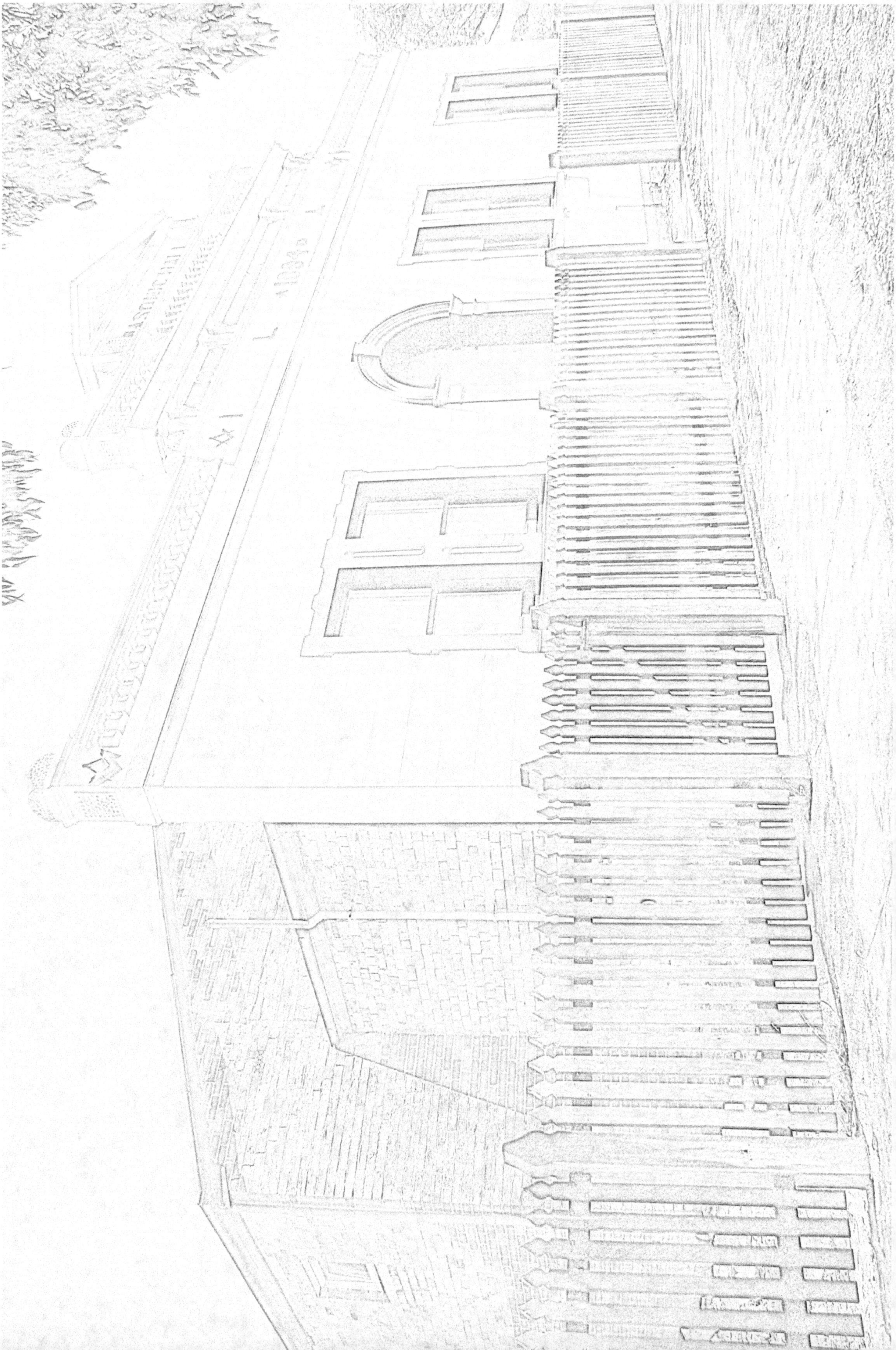

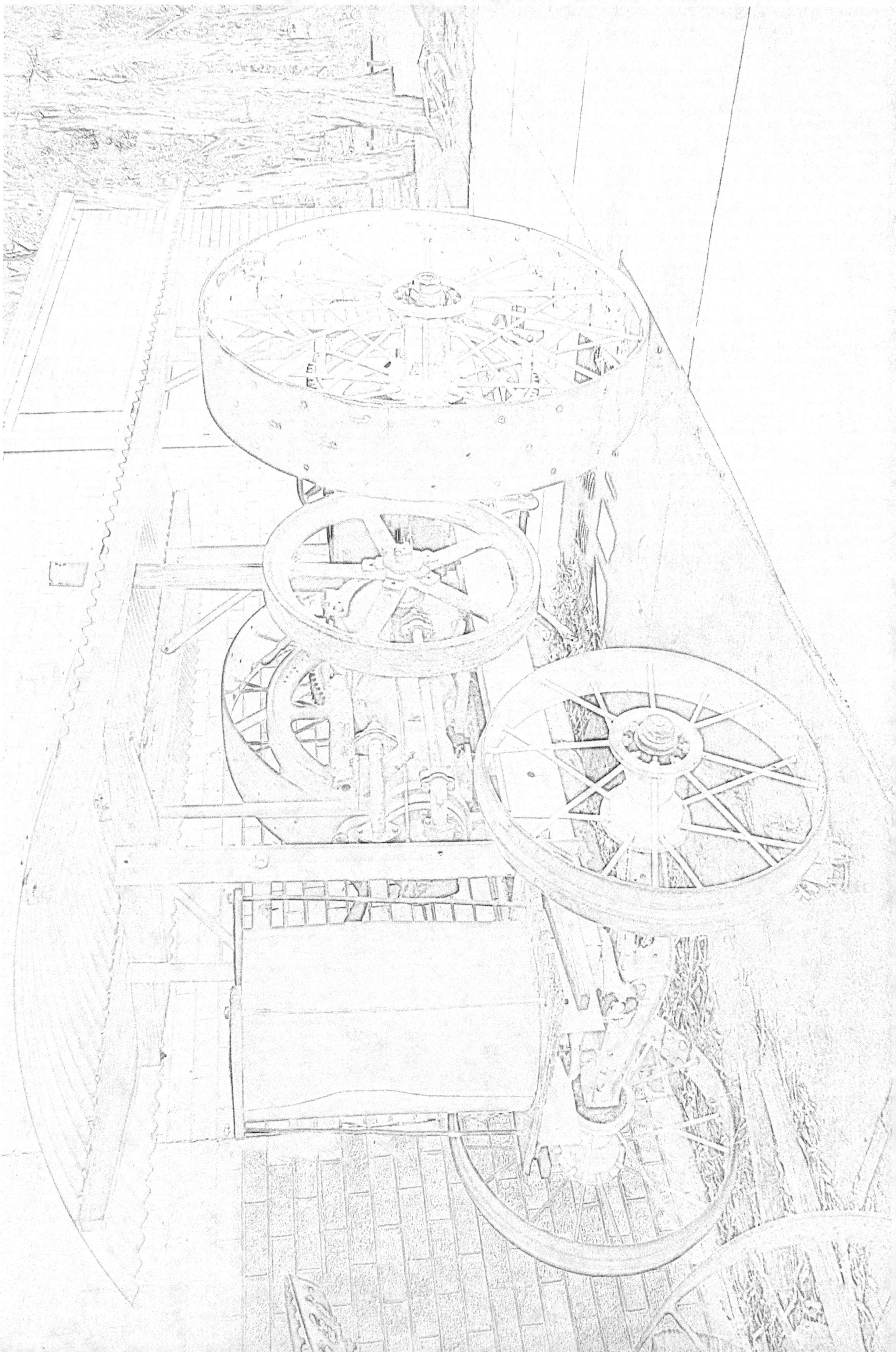

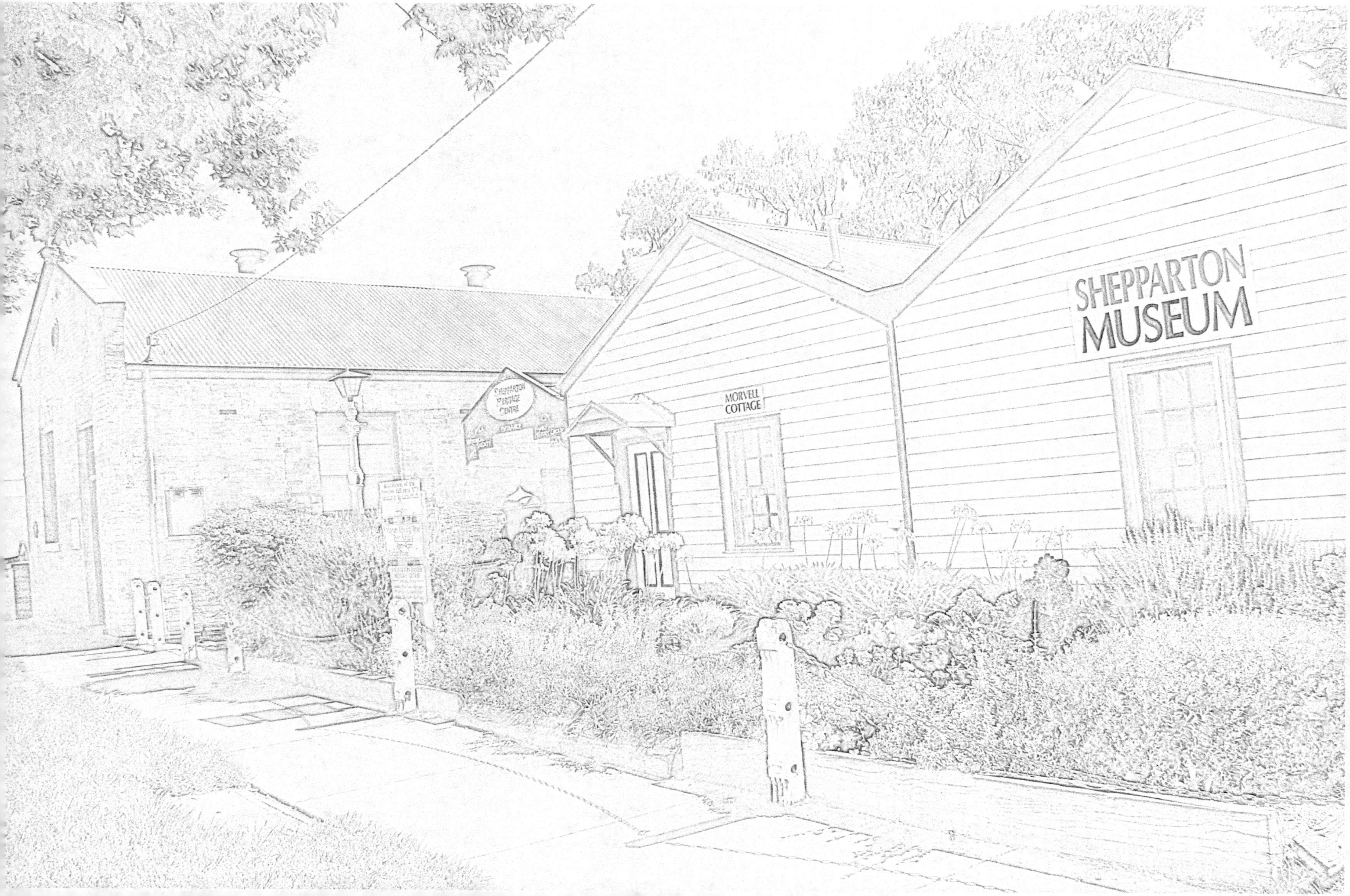
SHEPPARTON
MUSEUM
MORVELL
COTTAGE

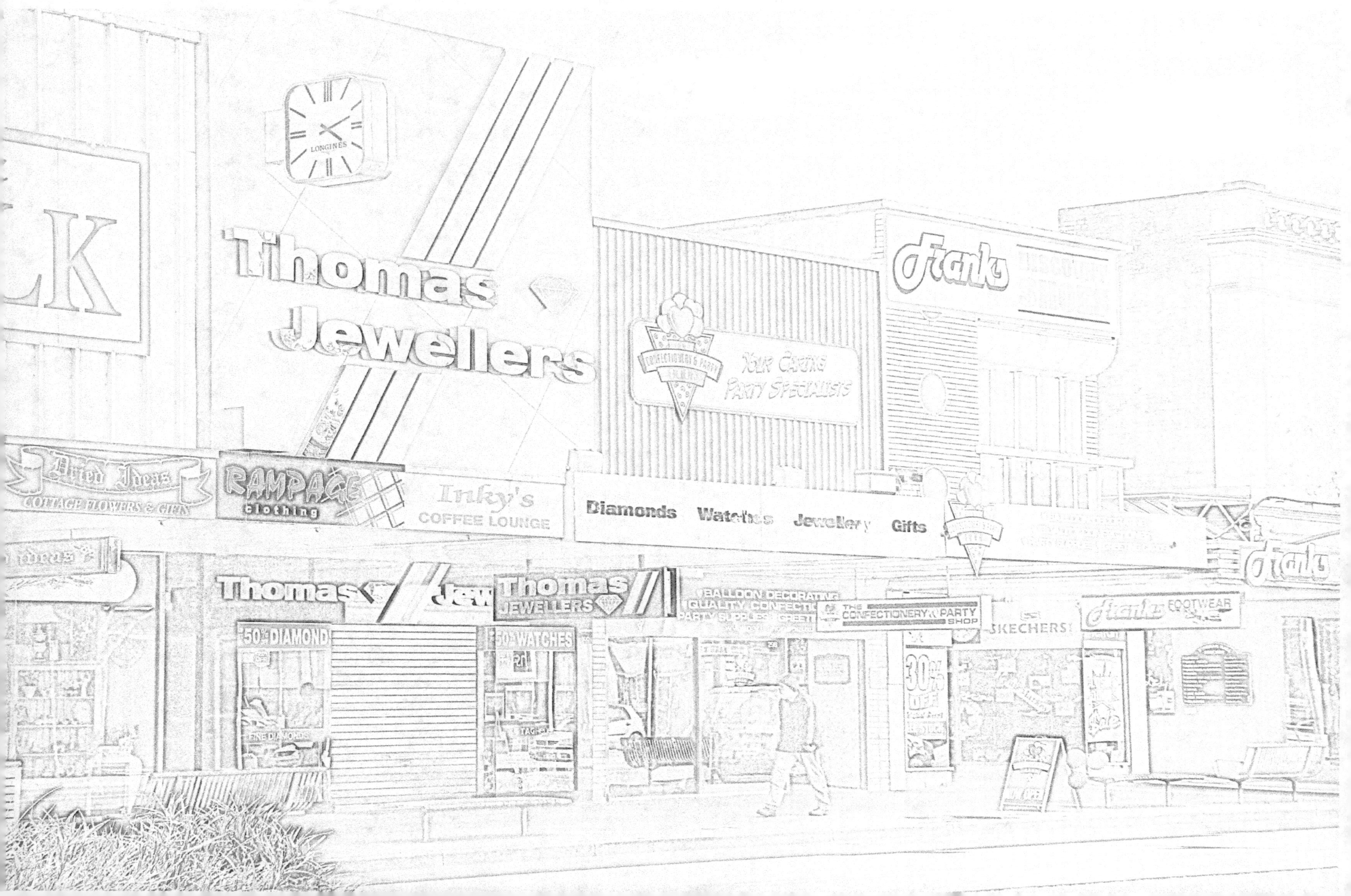
LONGINES
Thomas
Jewellers
Dried Ideas
COTTAGE FLOWERS & GIFTS
RAMPAGE
clothing
Inky's
COFFEE LOUNGE
Diamonds
Gifts
Franks
YOUR CARING
PARTY SPECIALISTS
Thomas
Thomas
JEWELLERS
50% DIAMOND
50% WATCHES
THE
CONFECTIONERY & PARTY
SHOP
SKECHERS
Franks
FOOTWEAR
30%
OFF

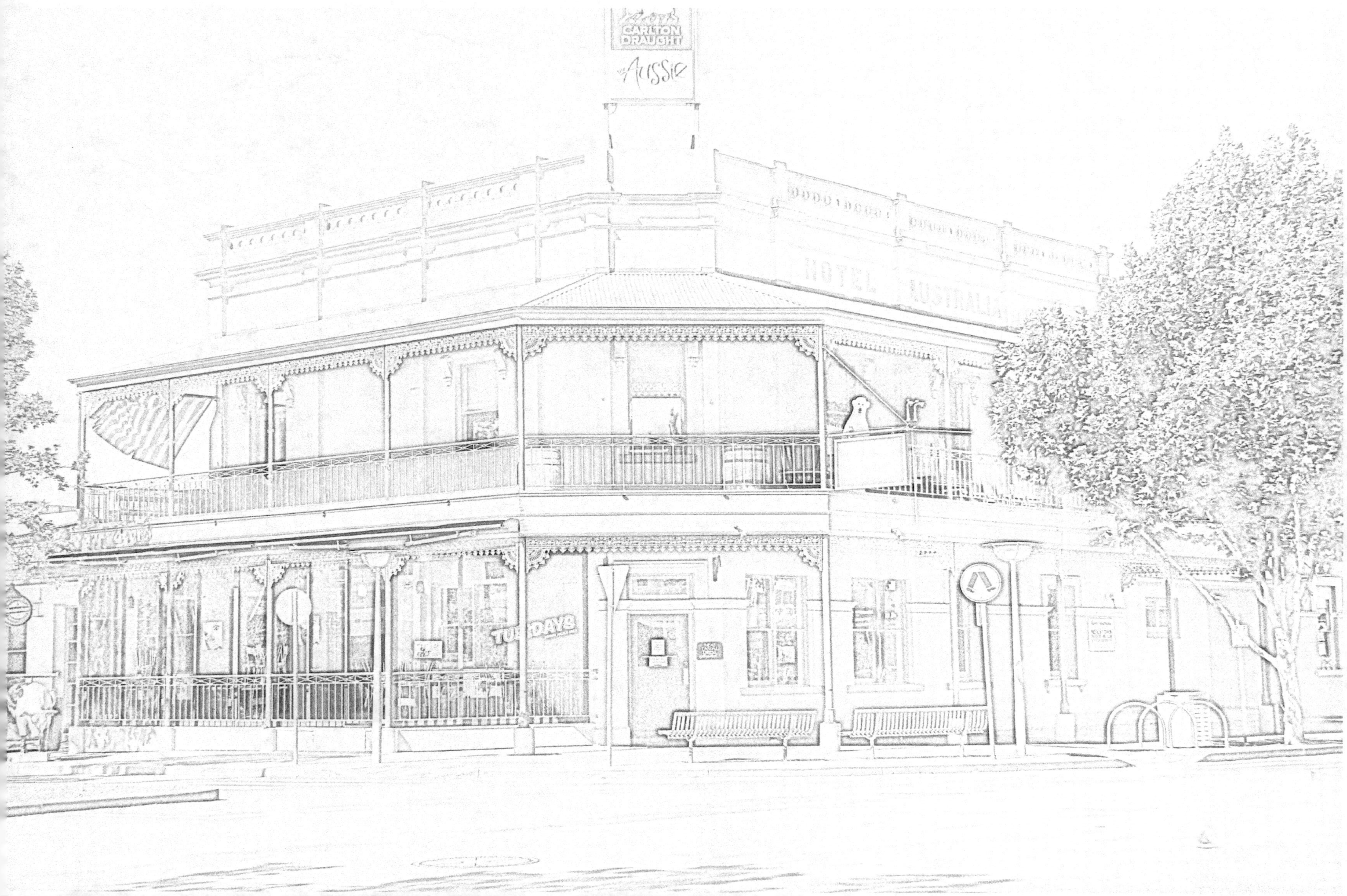
CARLTON DRAUGHT
Aussie
HOTEL AUSTRALIA
TUESDAYS

Rego
FLOUR
N. H.
MATHEWS
C.O.R
Agent
CRYSTALS

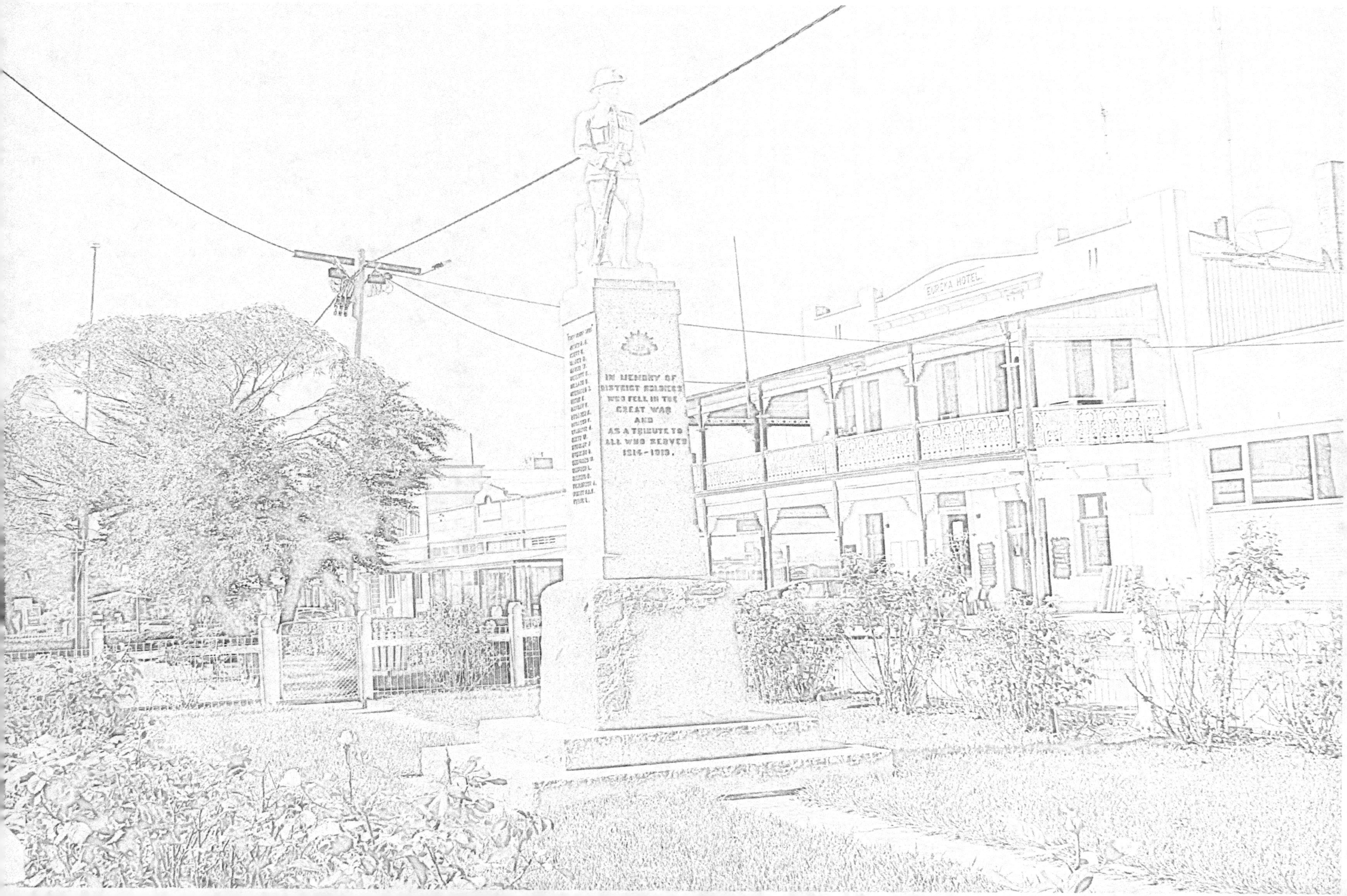
IN MEMORY OF
DISTRICT SOLDIERS
WHO FELL IN THE
GREAT WAR
AND
AS A TRIBUTE TO
ALL WHO SERVED
1914-1919.
EUREKA HOTEL.

EUREKA HOTEL.
EUREKA HOTEL.
Eureka Hotel
DISCOUNT LIQUOR
MEALS DAYS ACCOMMODATION
HOSPITAL
POLICE

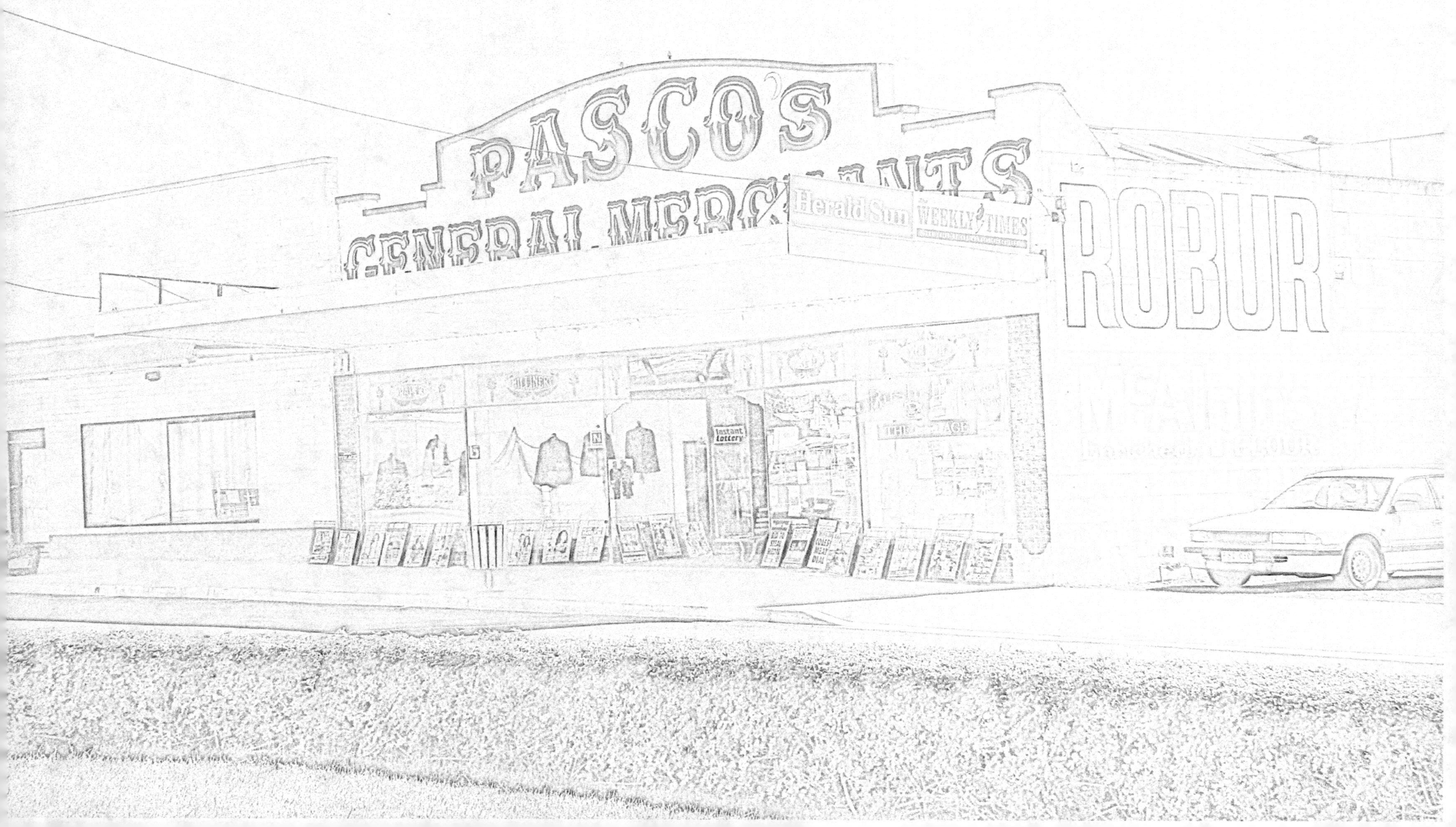
PASCO'S
Herald Sun
WEEKLY TIMES
ROBUR
Instant Lottery

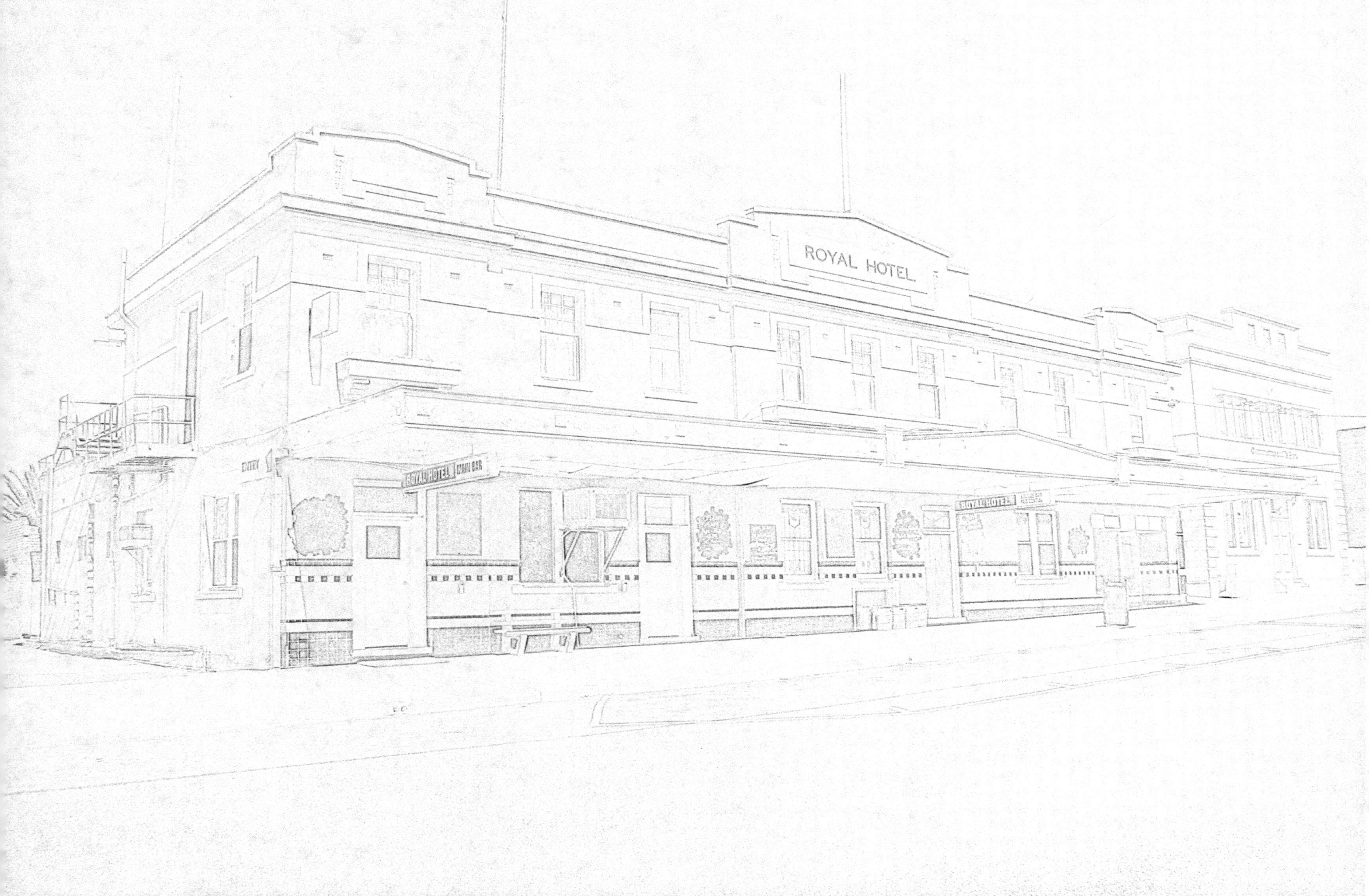
ROYAL HOTEL
ROYAL HOTEL
ROYAL HOTEL

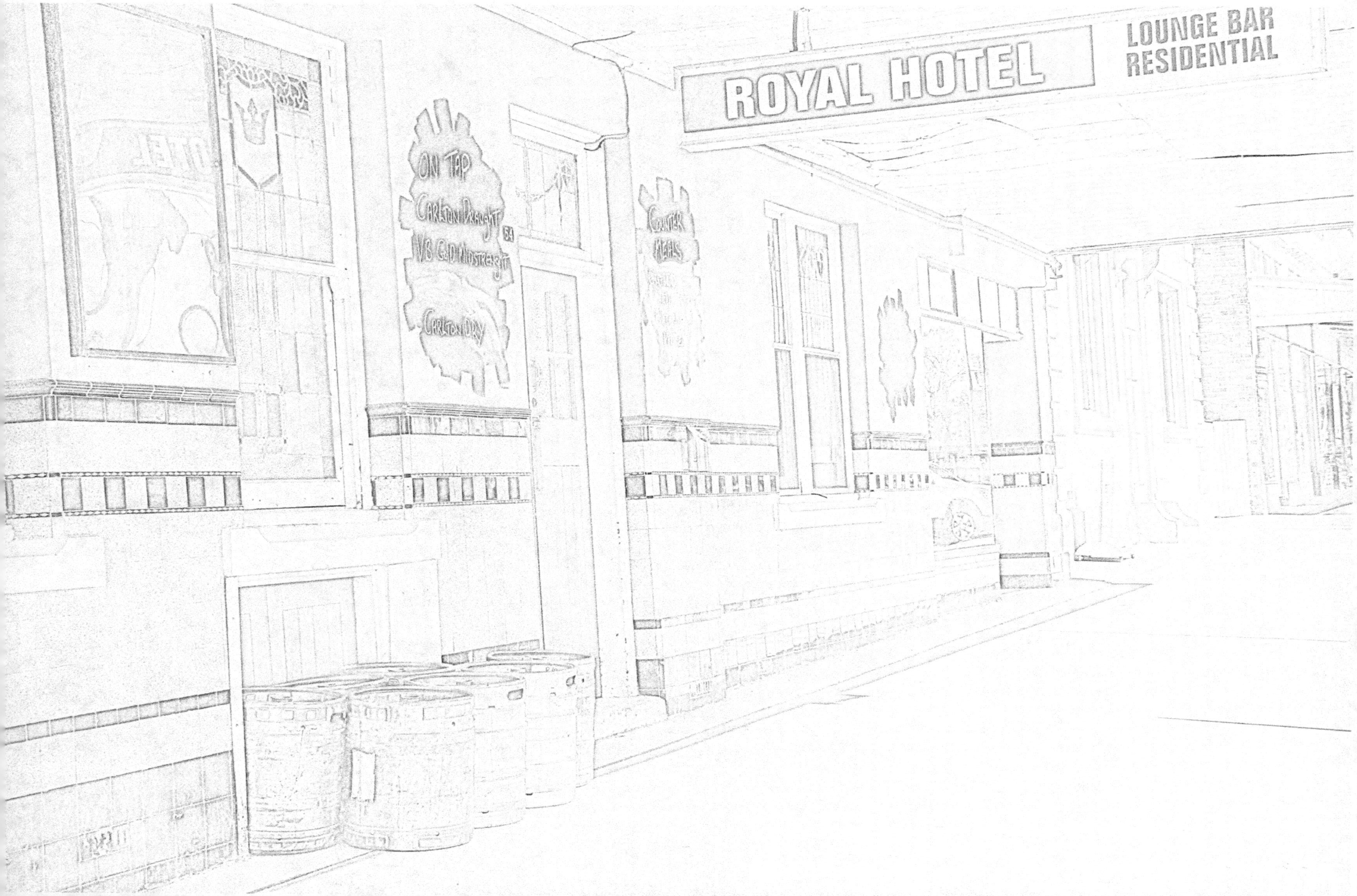
ROYAL HOTEL
LOUNGE BAR
RESIDENTIAL
ON TAP
CARLTON DRAUGHT
CARLTON DRY
COUNTER MEALS

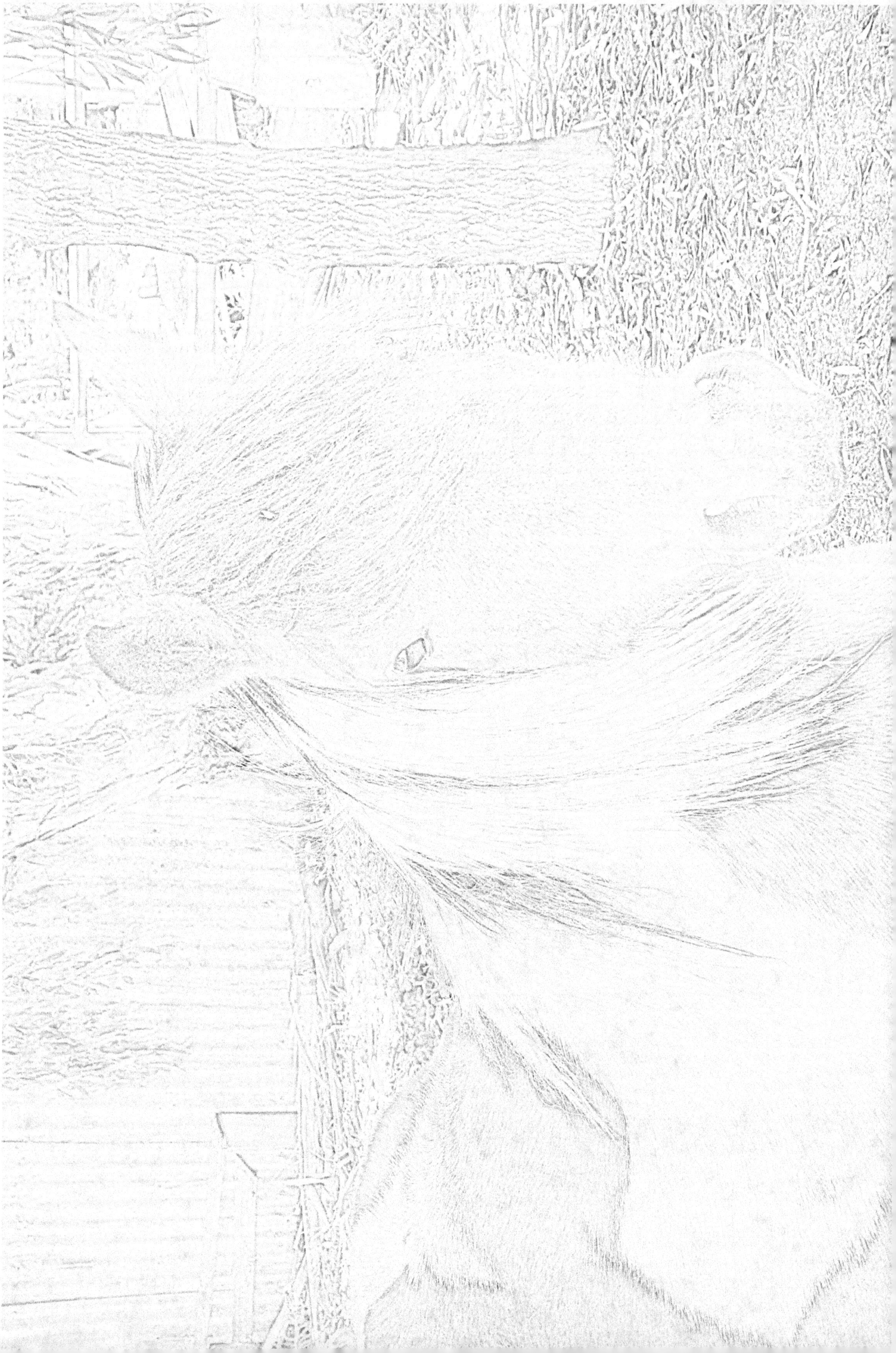

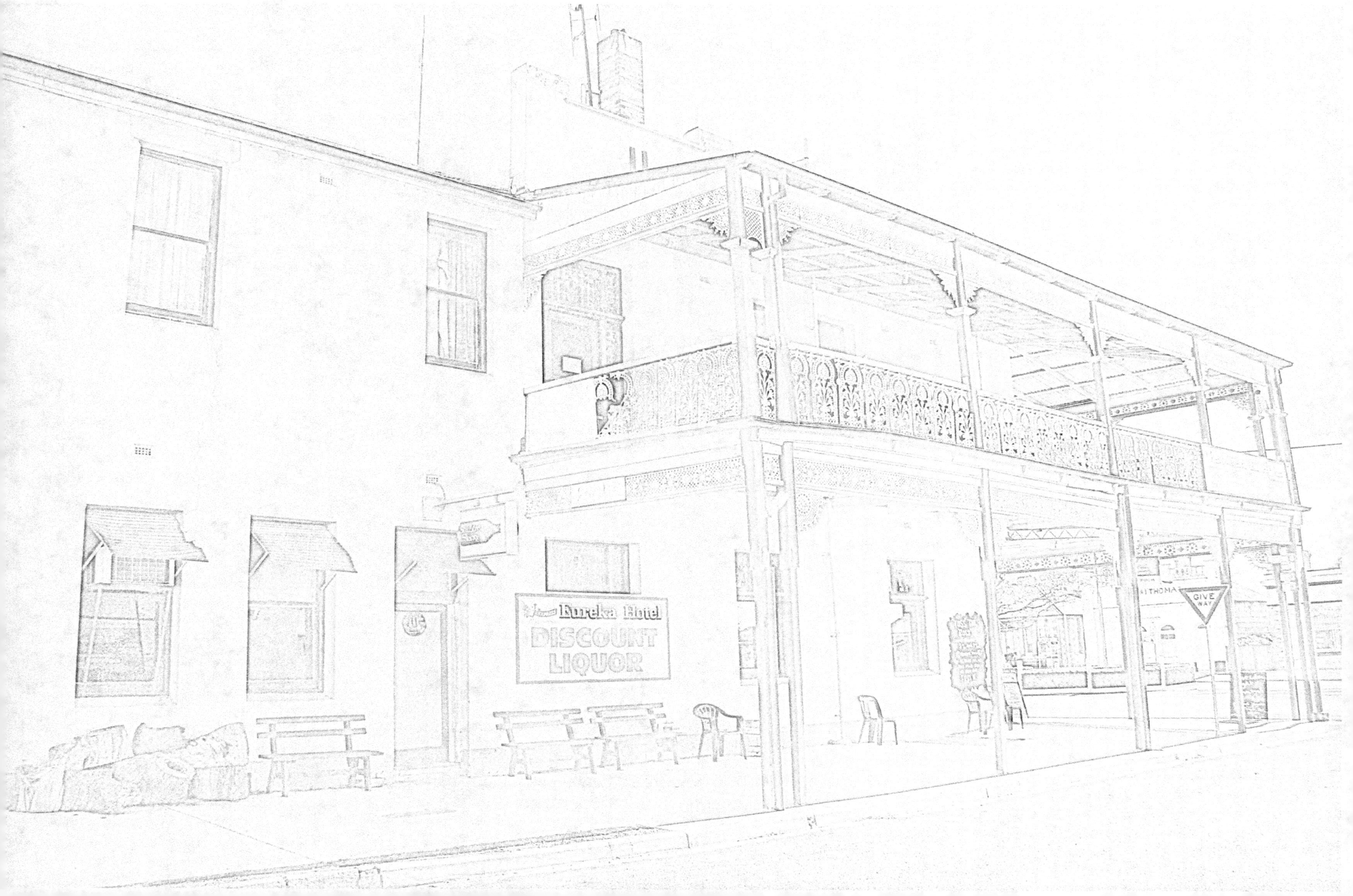
Eureka Hotel
DISCOUNT
LIQUOR
GIVE WAY

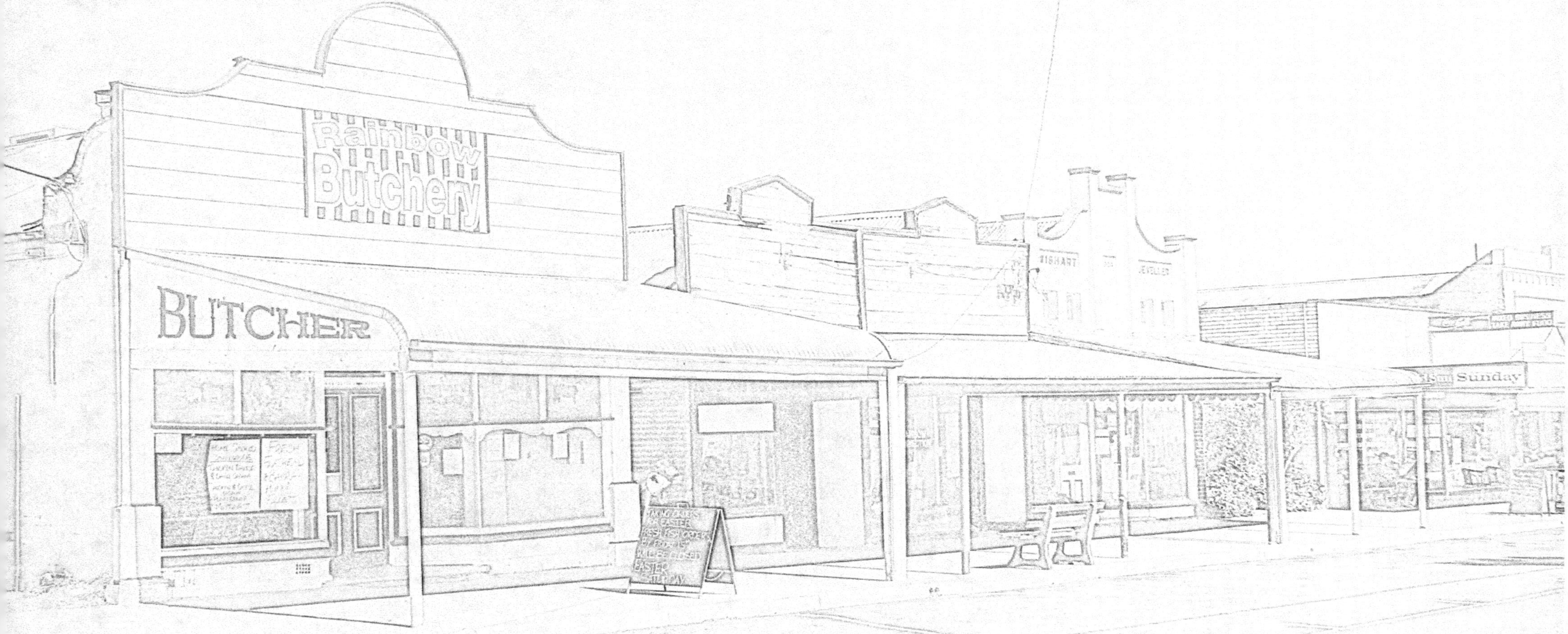
Rainbow Butchery
BUTCHER
WISHART
JEWELLER
Sunday

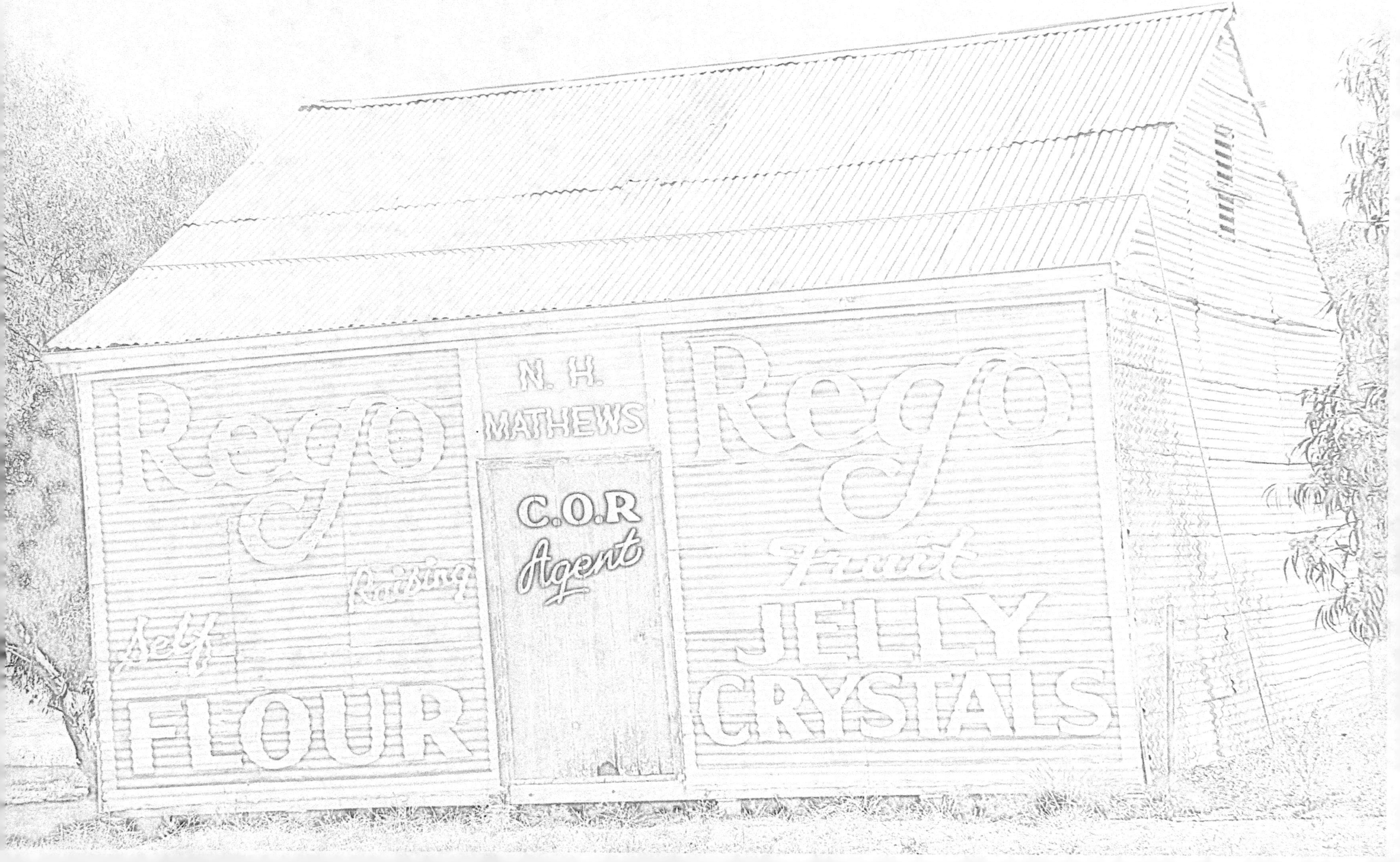
Rego
Self Raising
FLOUR
N. H.
MATHEWS
C.O.R
Agent
Rego
Fruit
JELLY
CRYSTALS

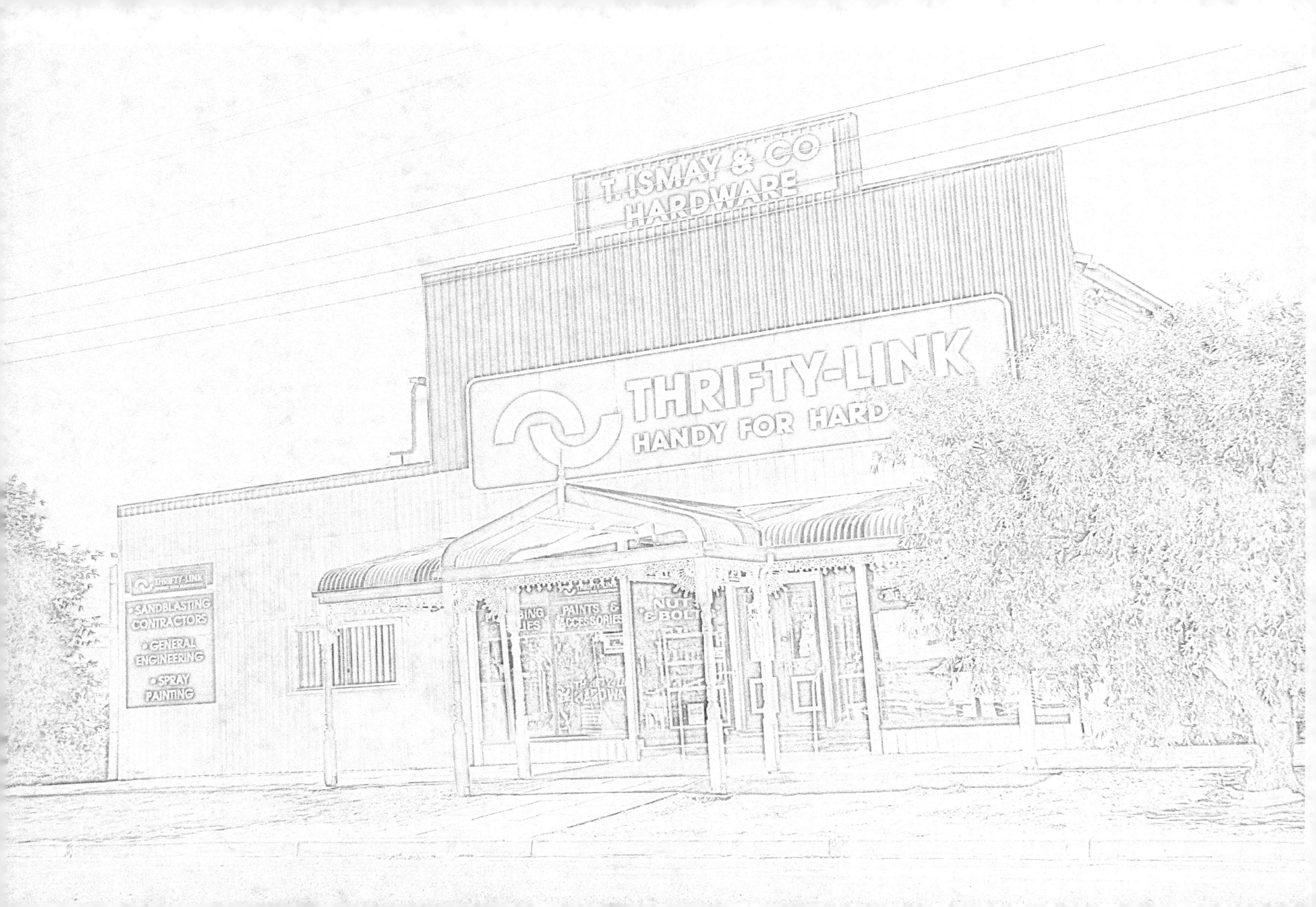
T. ISMAY & CO
HARDWARE
THRIFTY-LINK
HANDY FOR HARD
THRIFTY-LINK
• SANDBLASTING CONTRACTORS
• GENERAL ENGINEERING
• SPRAY PAINTING
PAINTS & ACCESSORIES

Sunshine
Sunshine

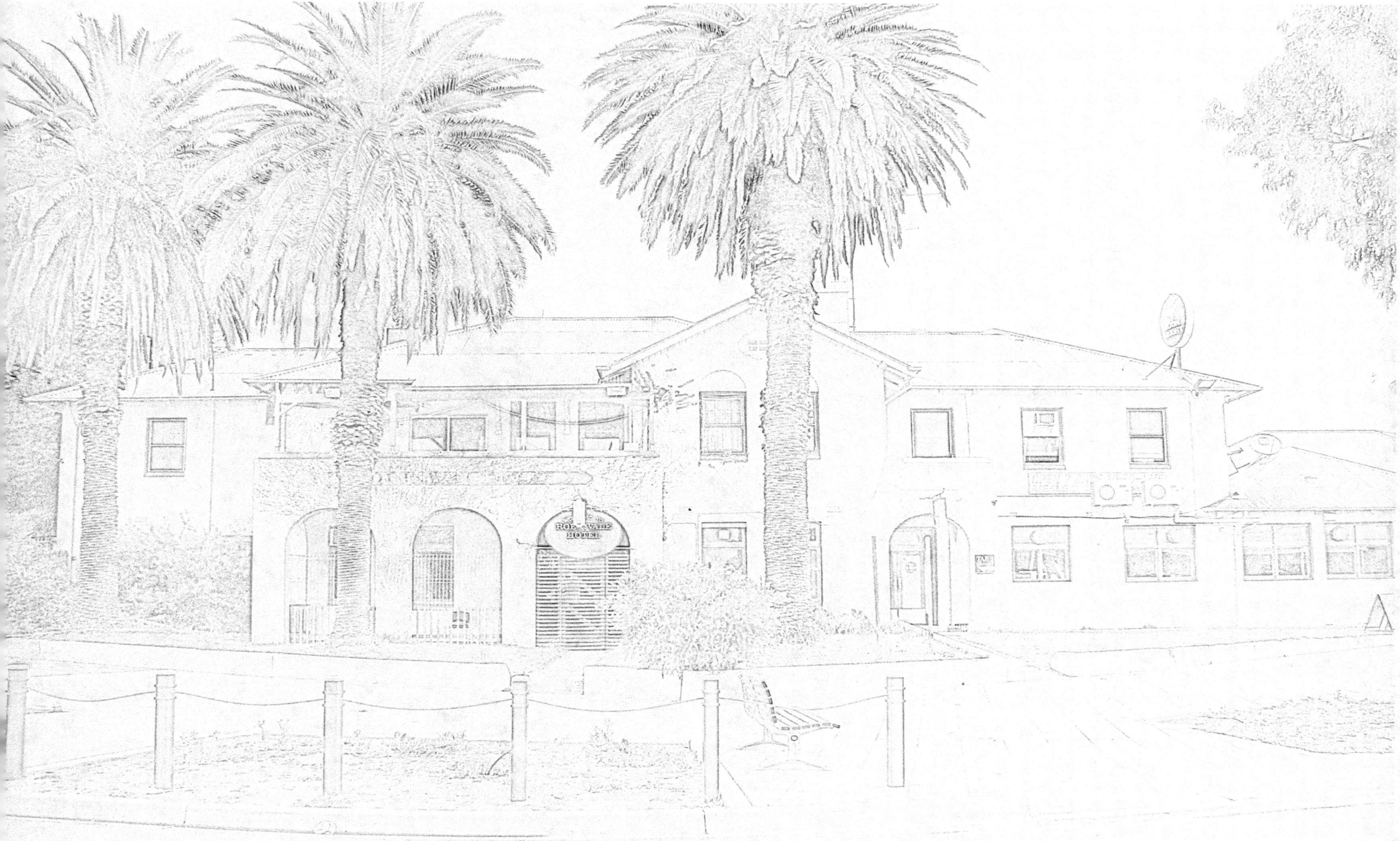
HOTEL

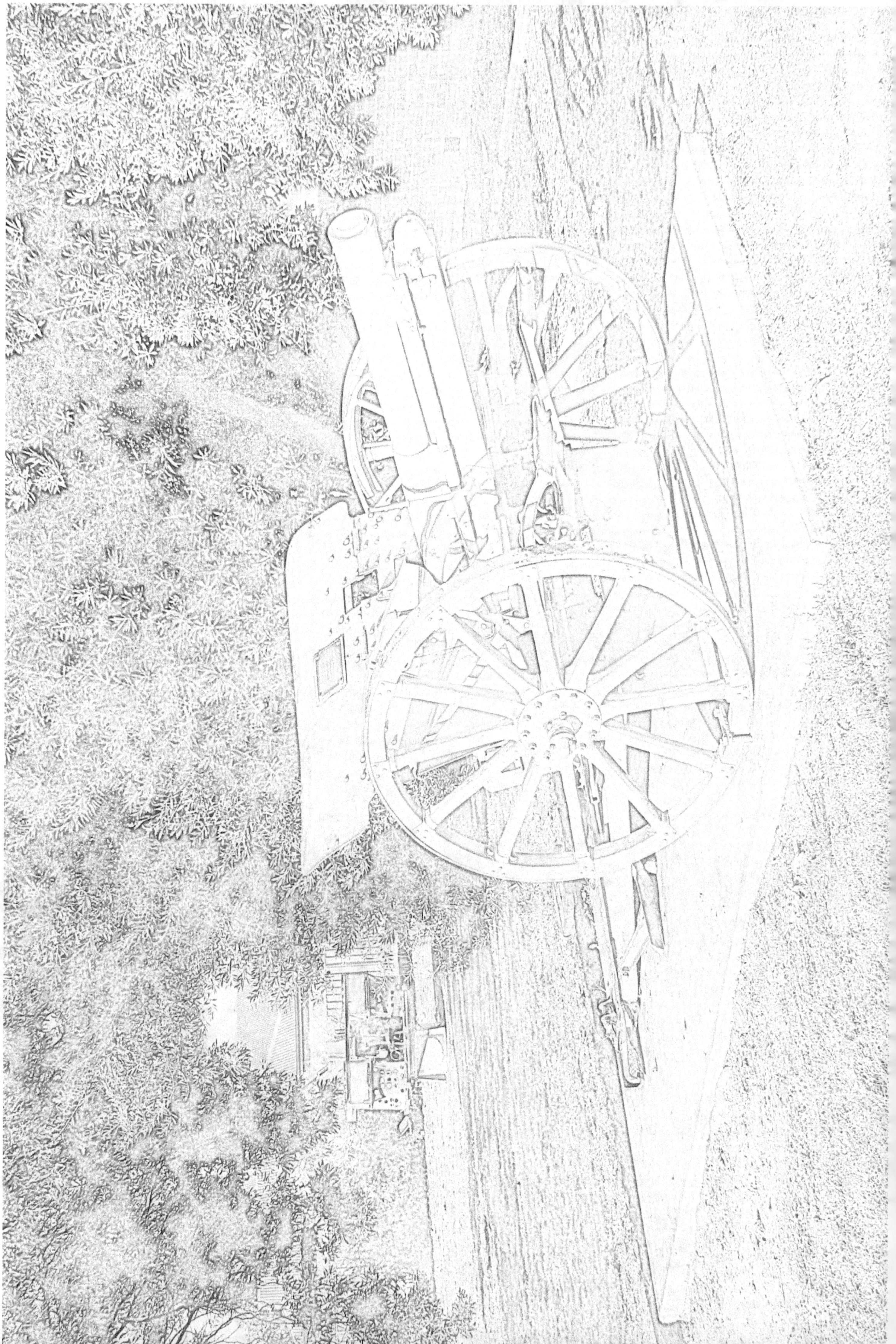

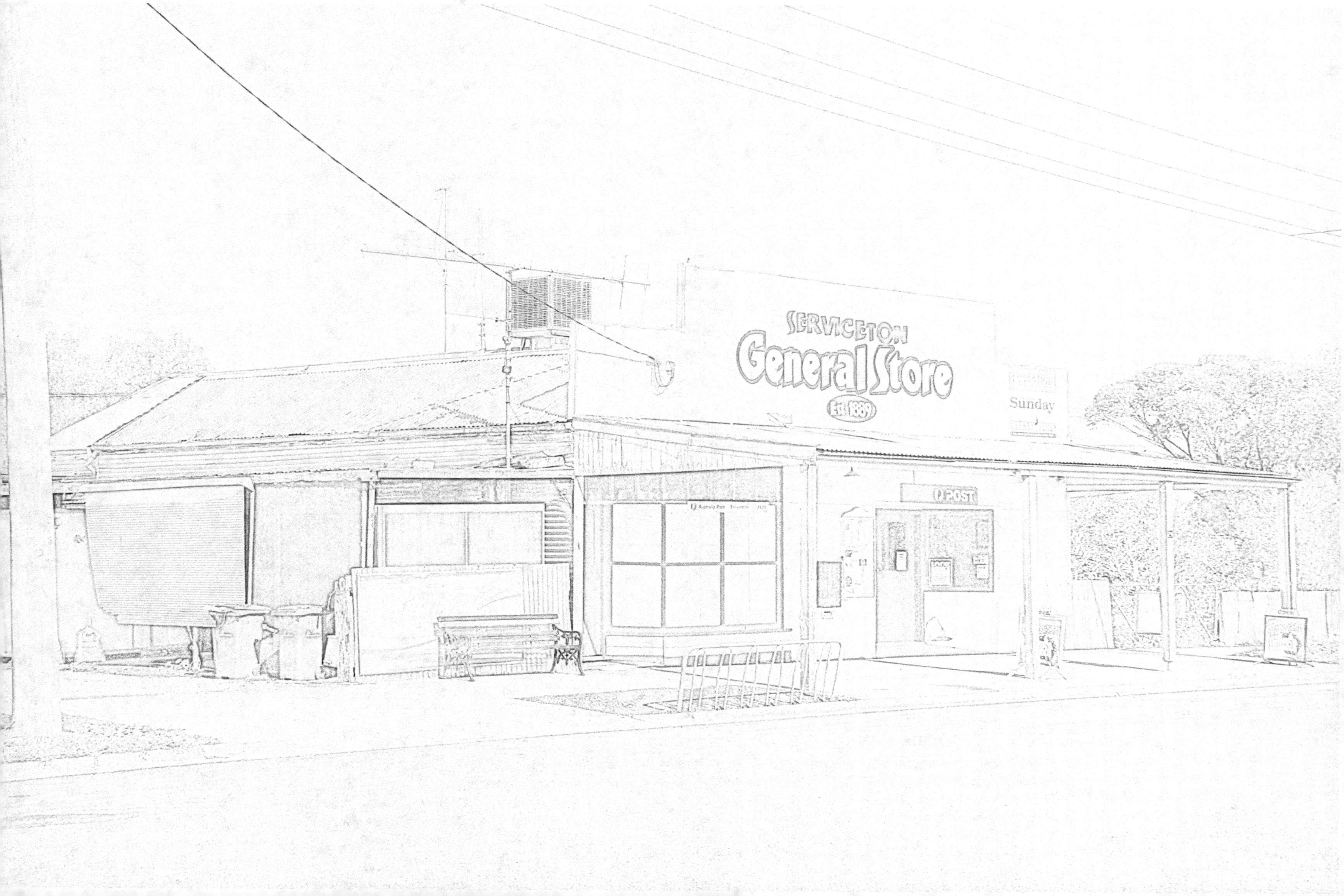
SERVICETON
General Store
Est 1889
Sunday
POST

EIIR
POST
RUPANYUP
POST OFFICE

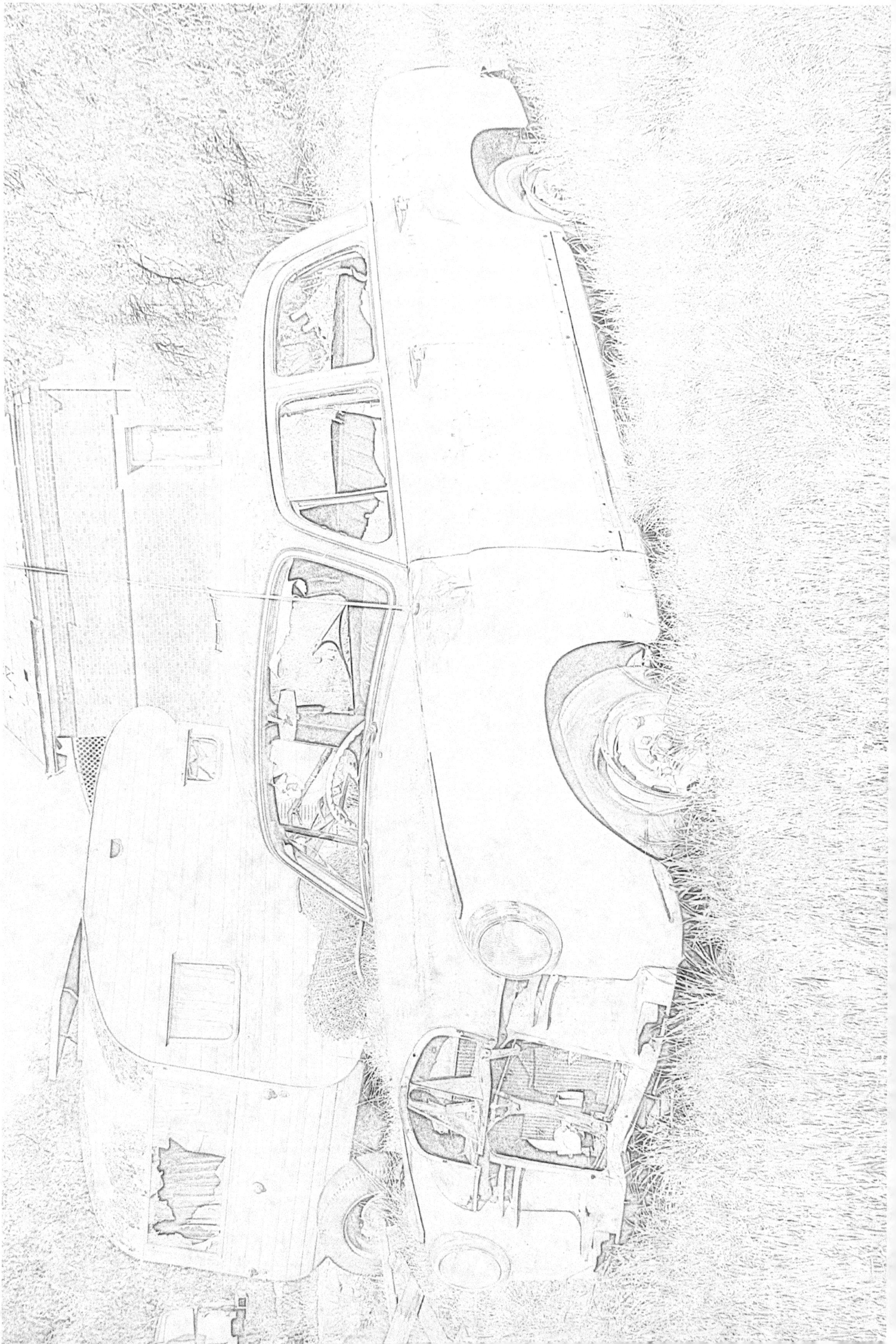

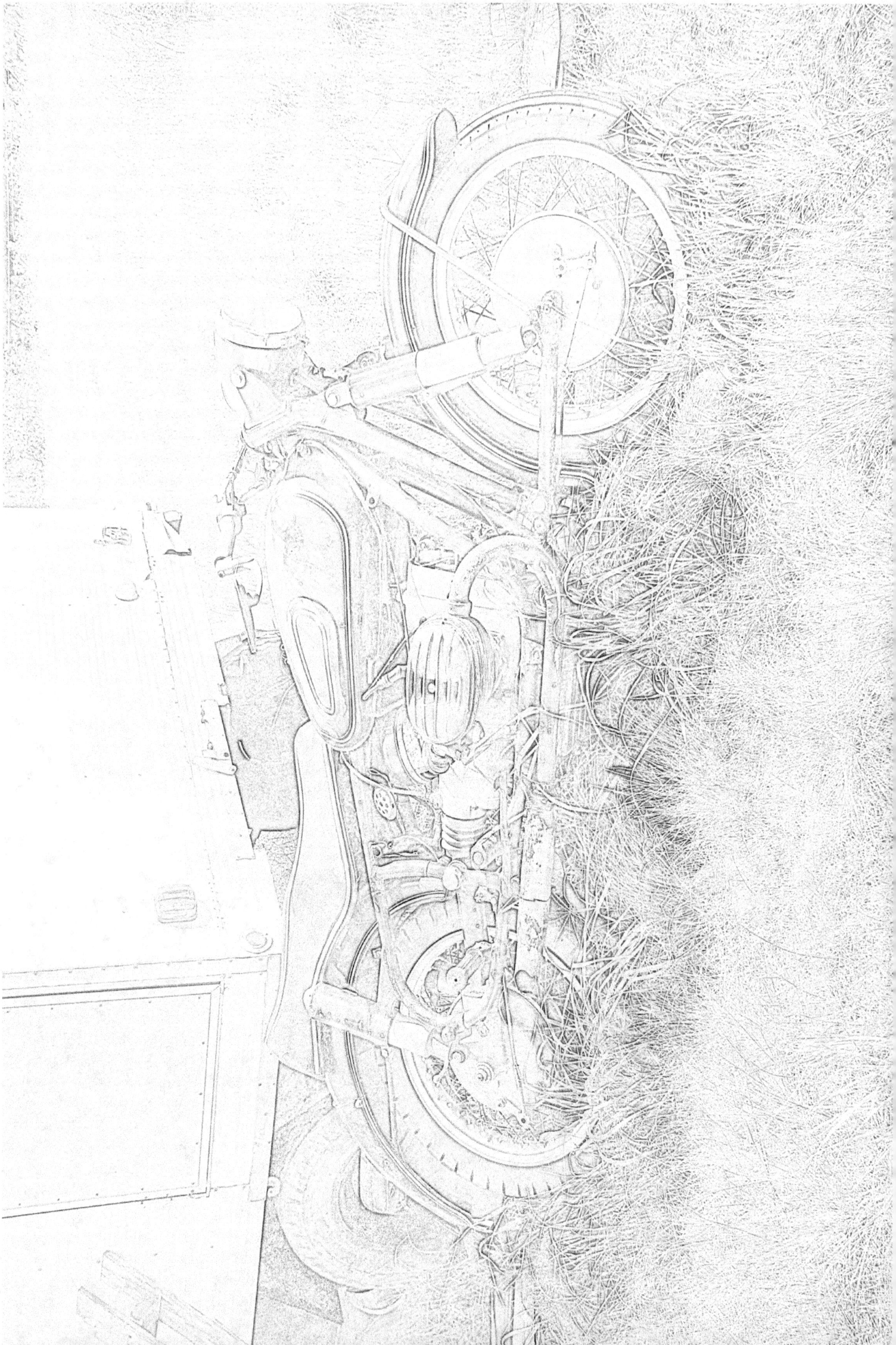

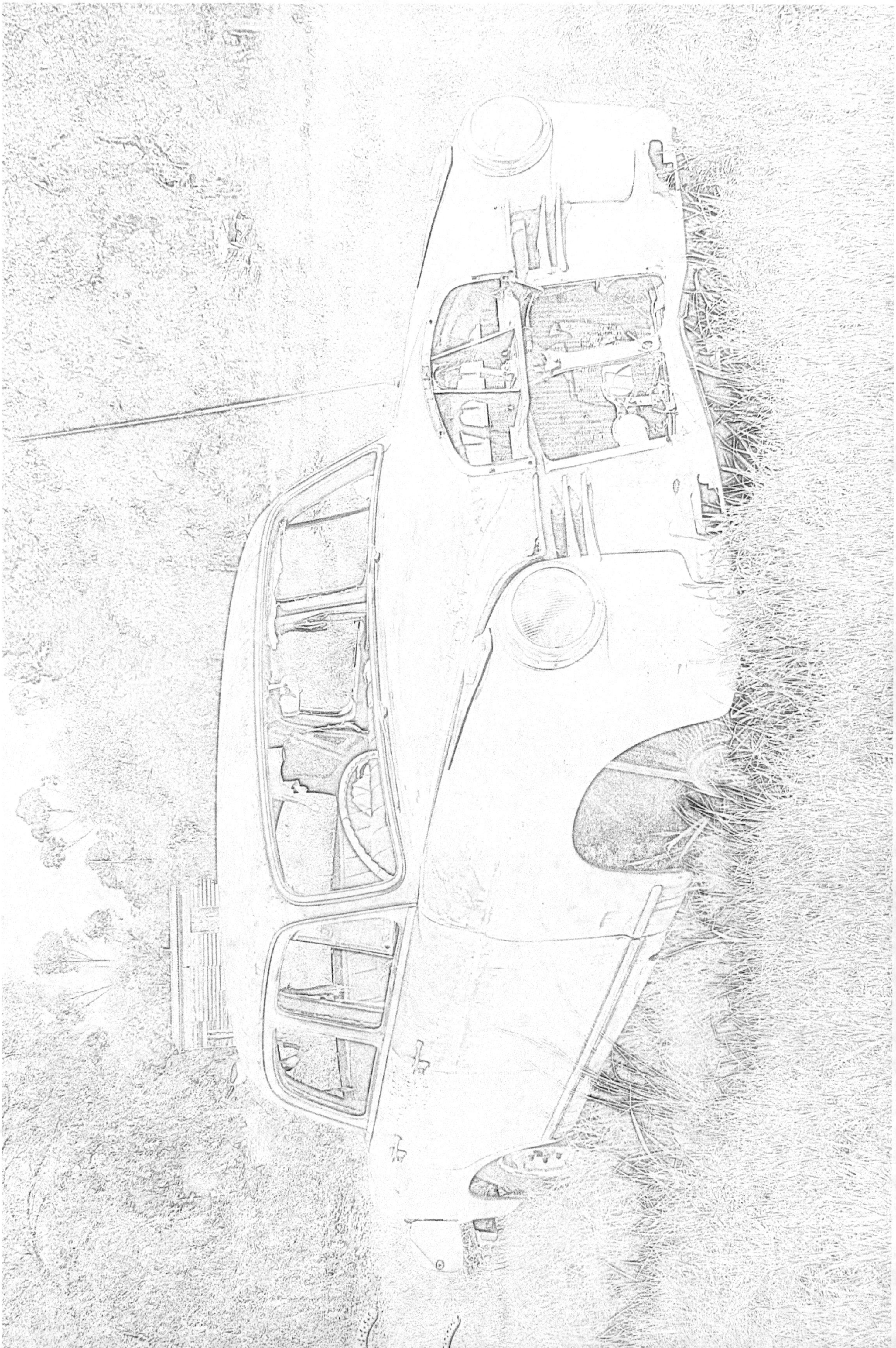

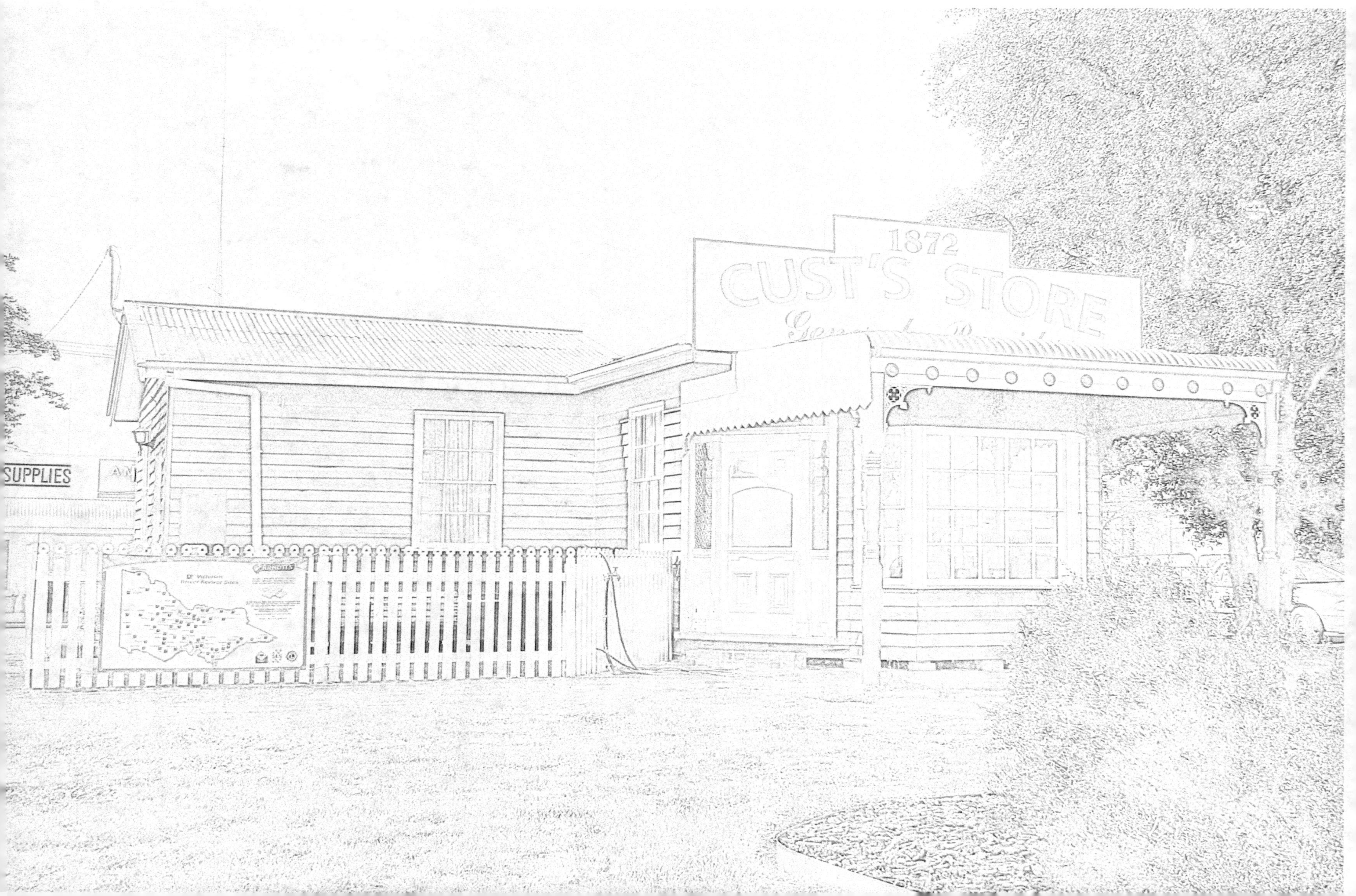
1872
CUST'S STORE
SUPPLIES
ARNOTTS

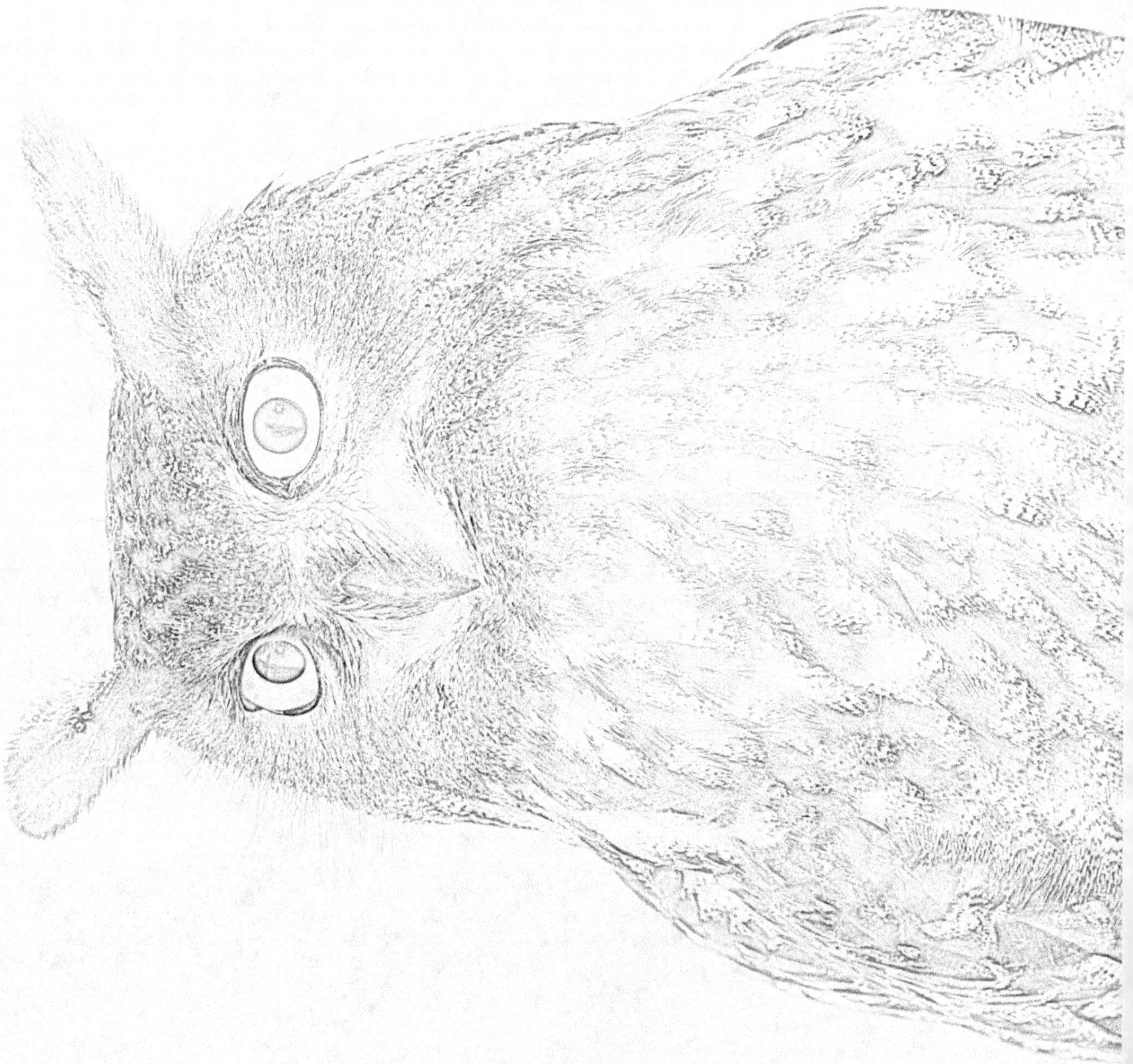

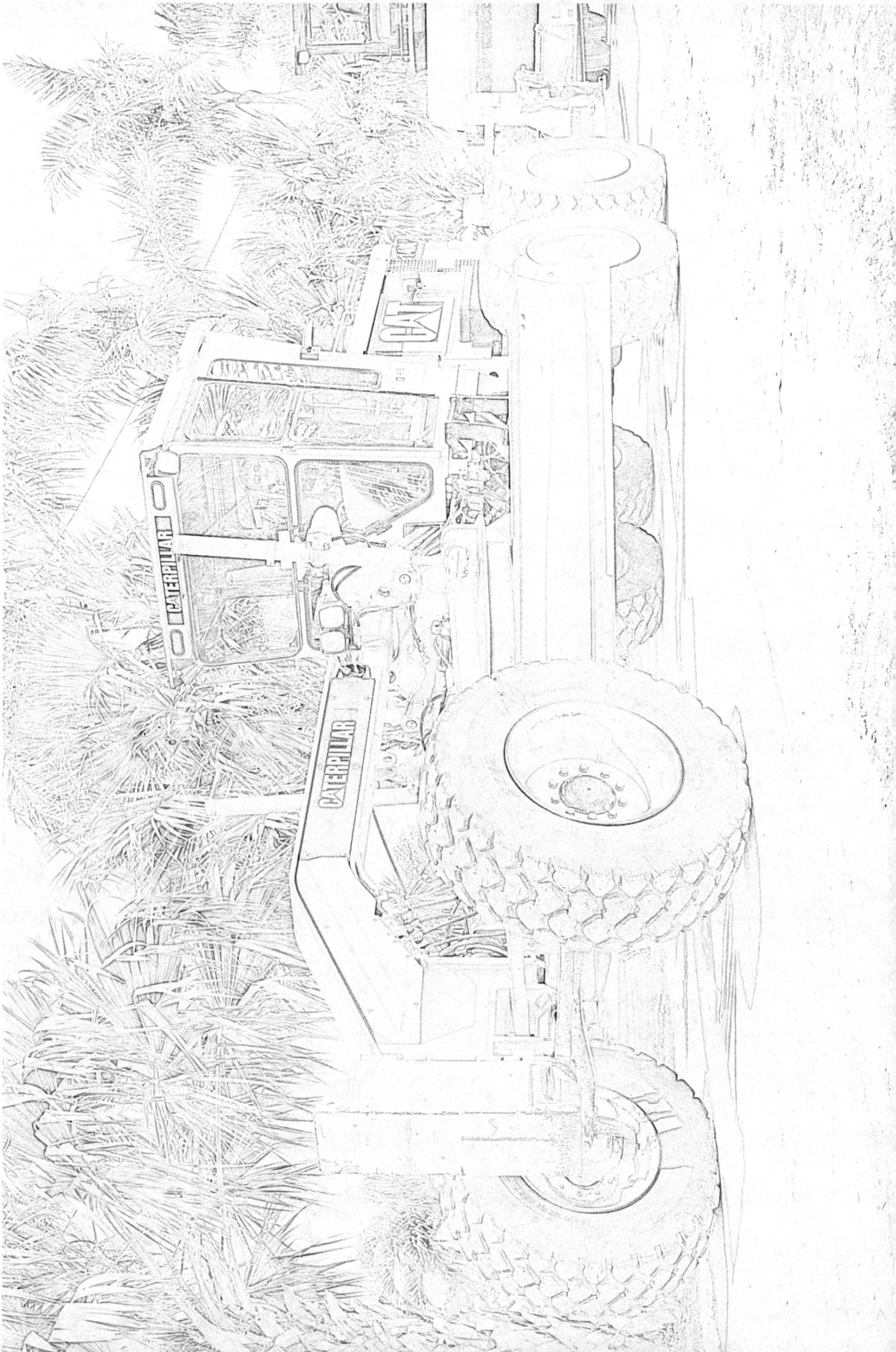
CATERPILLAR
CATERPILLAR
CAT

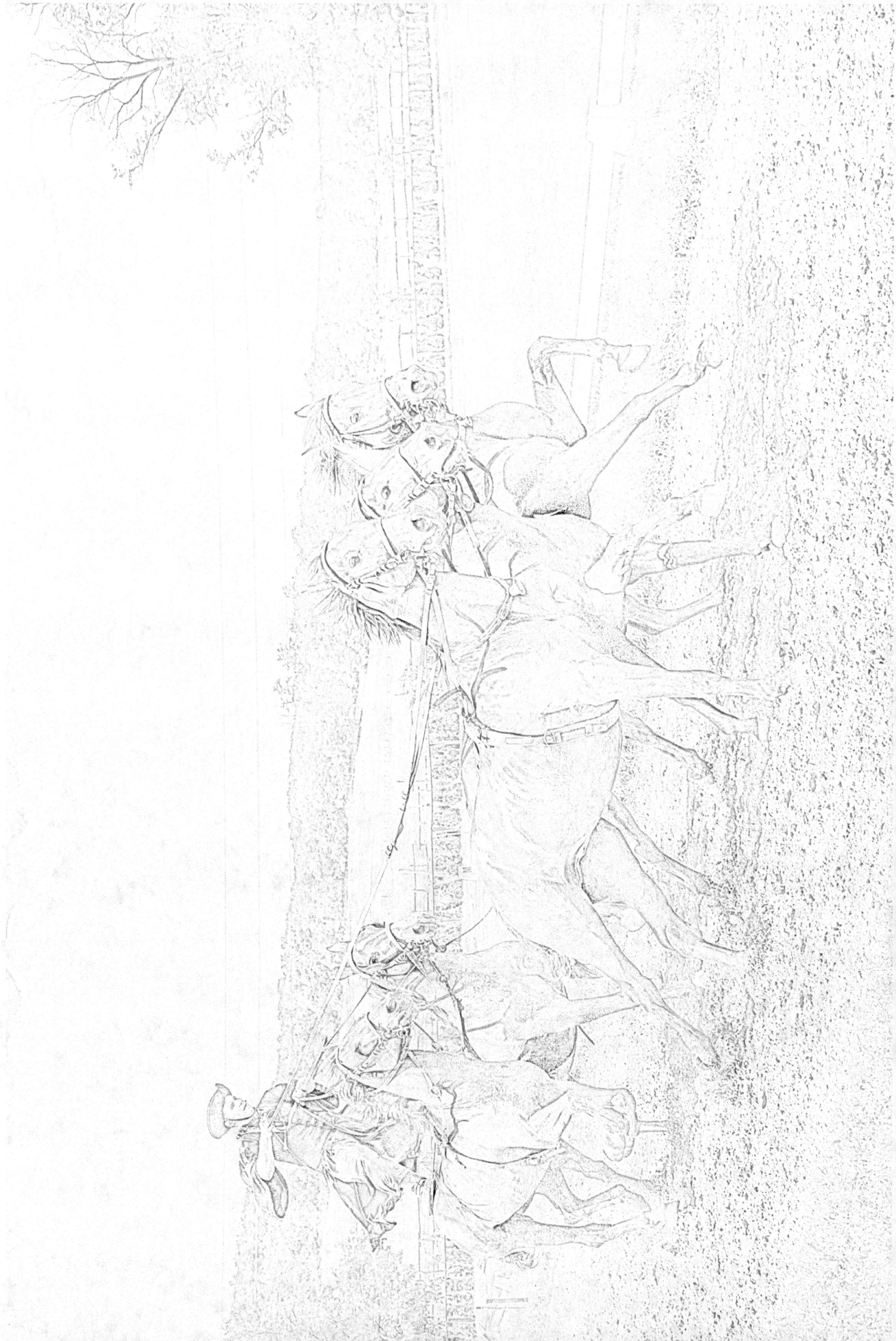

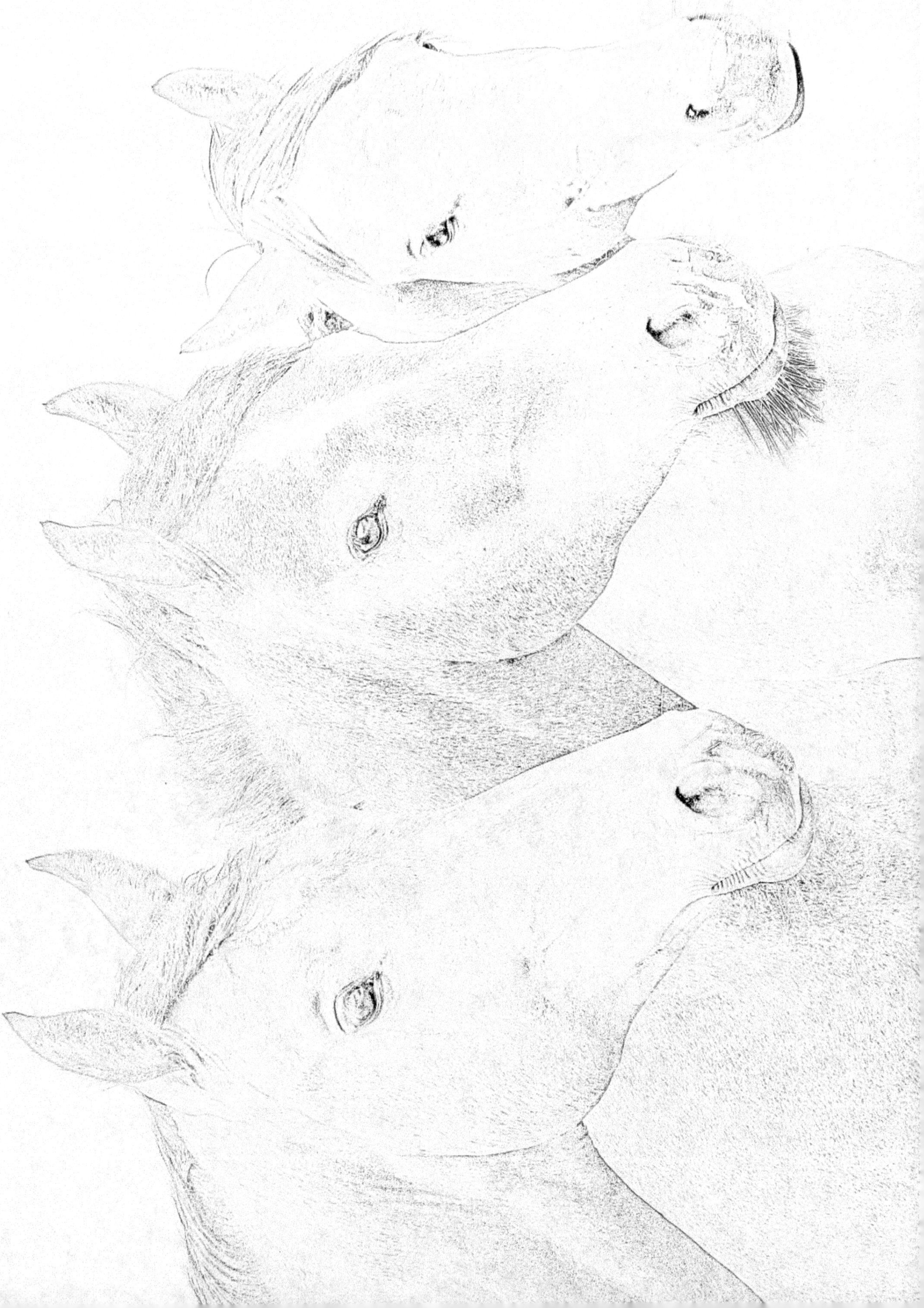

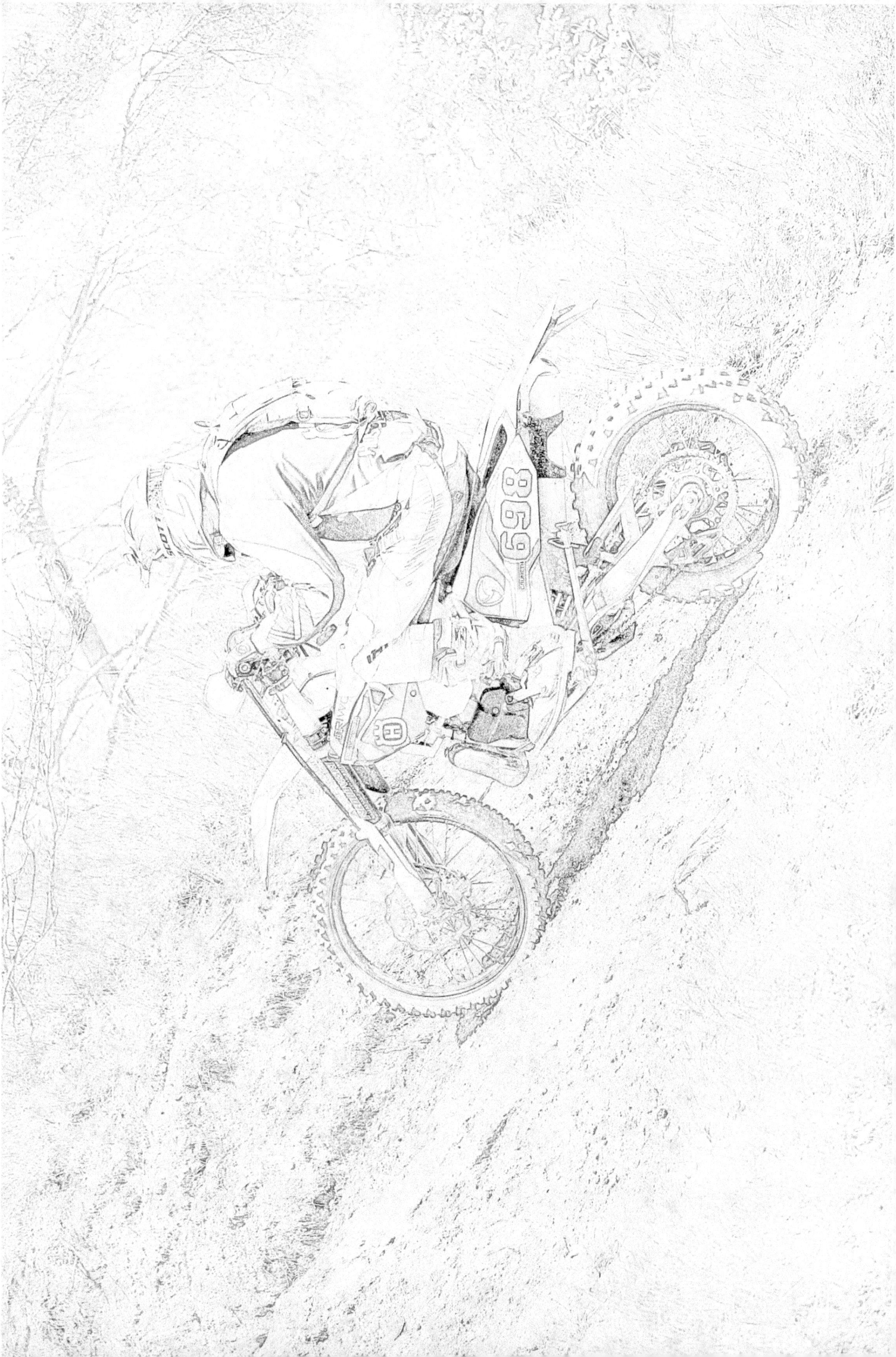

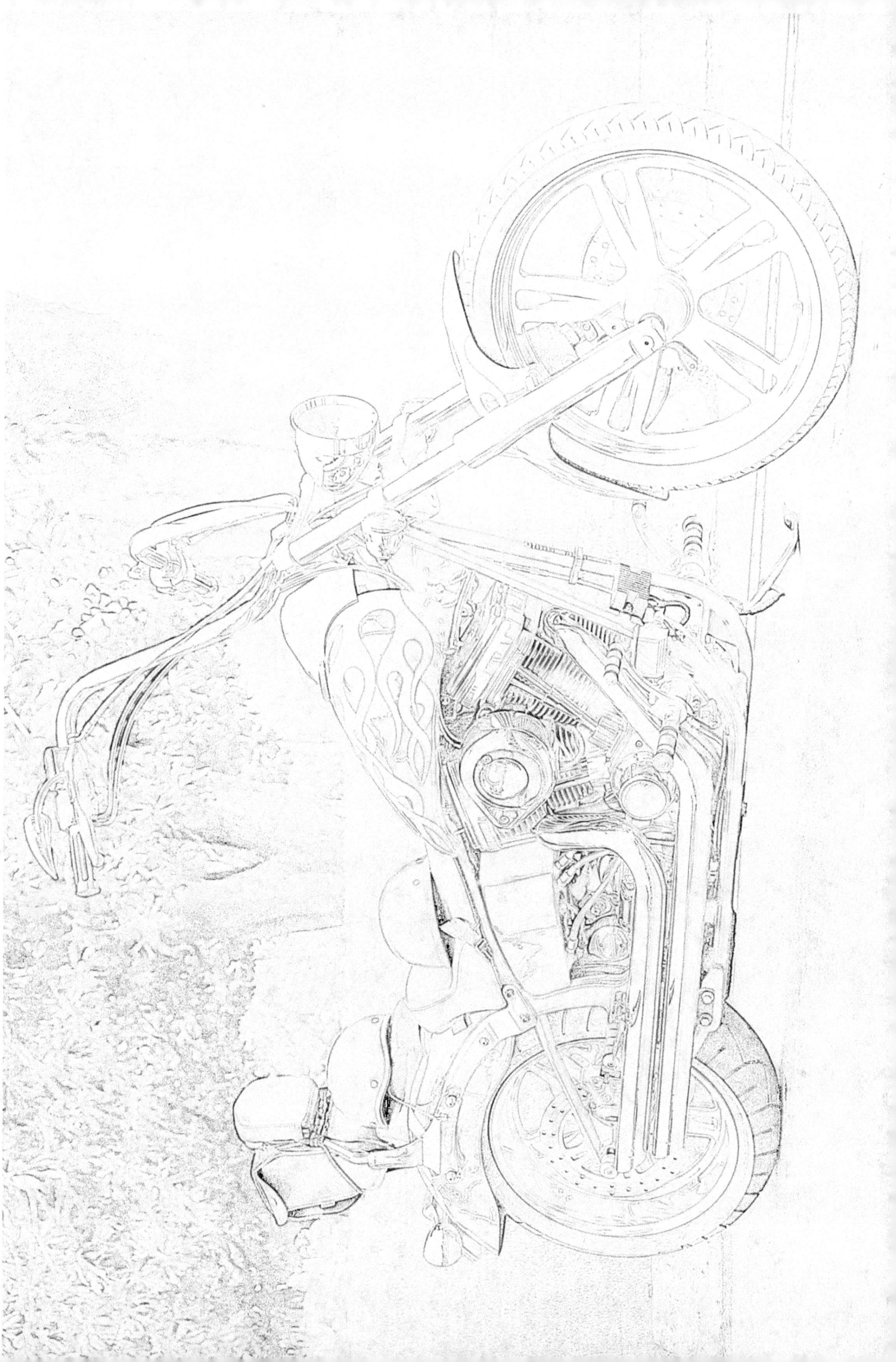

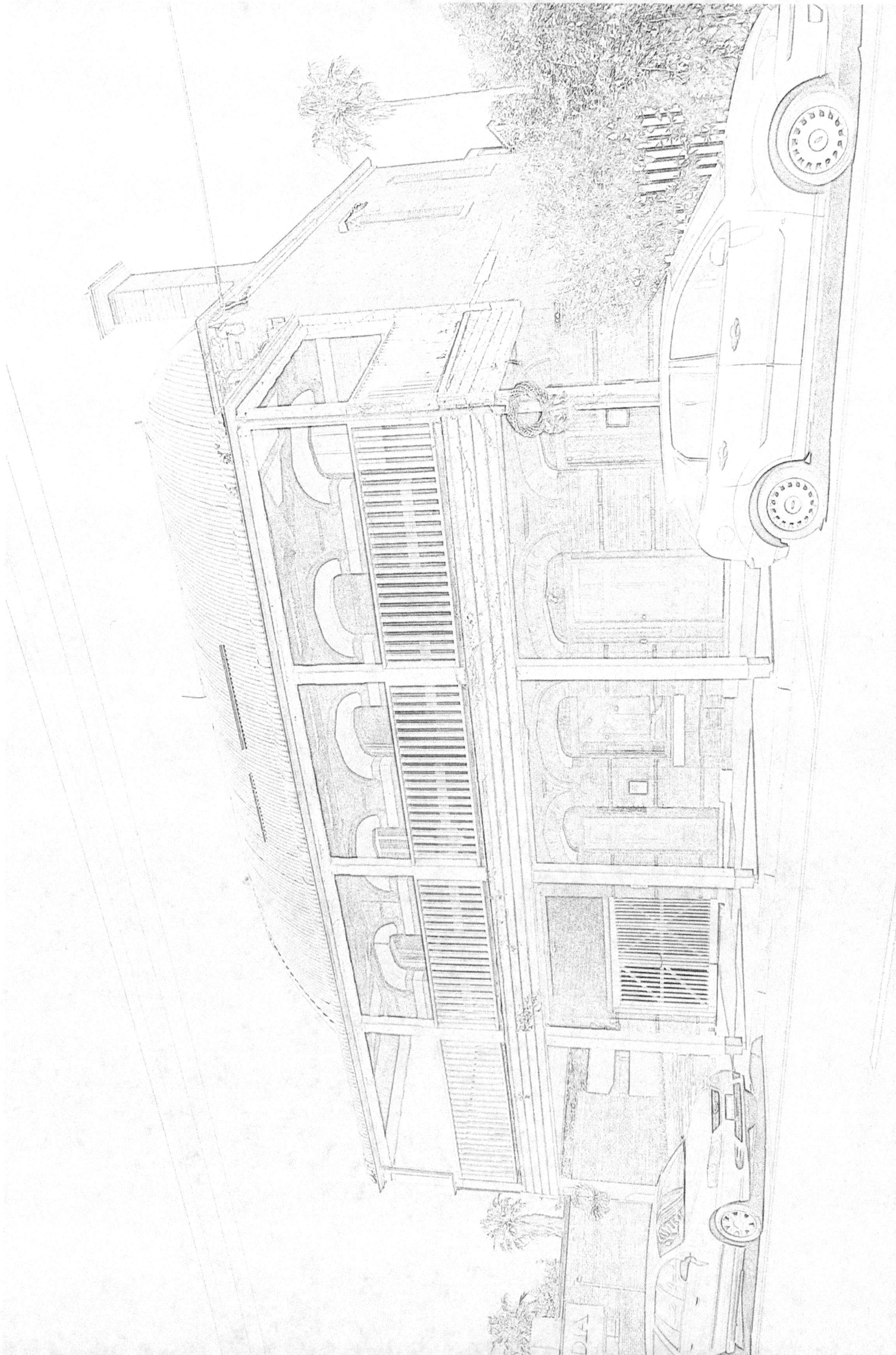

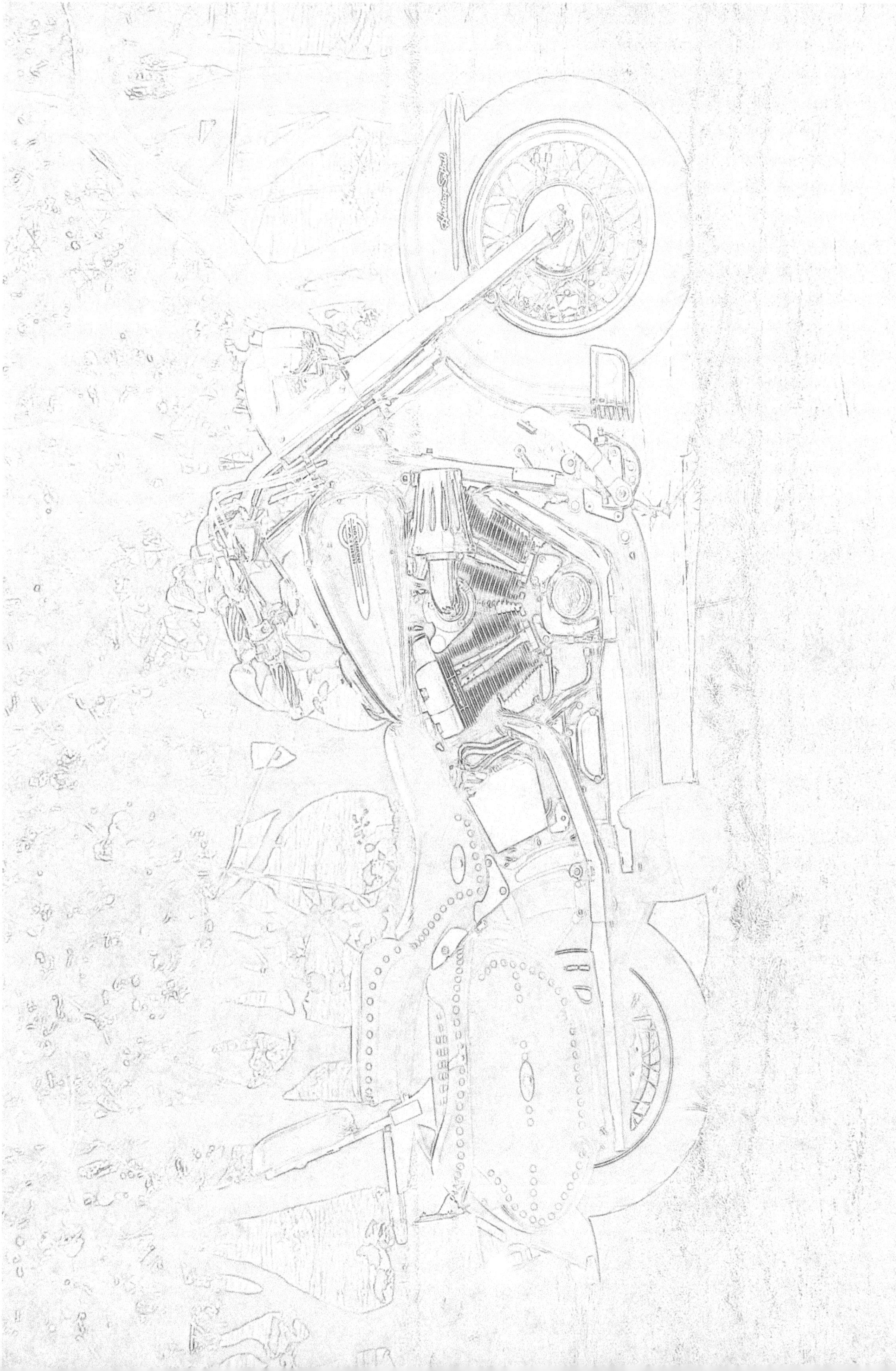

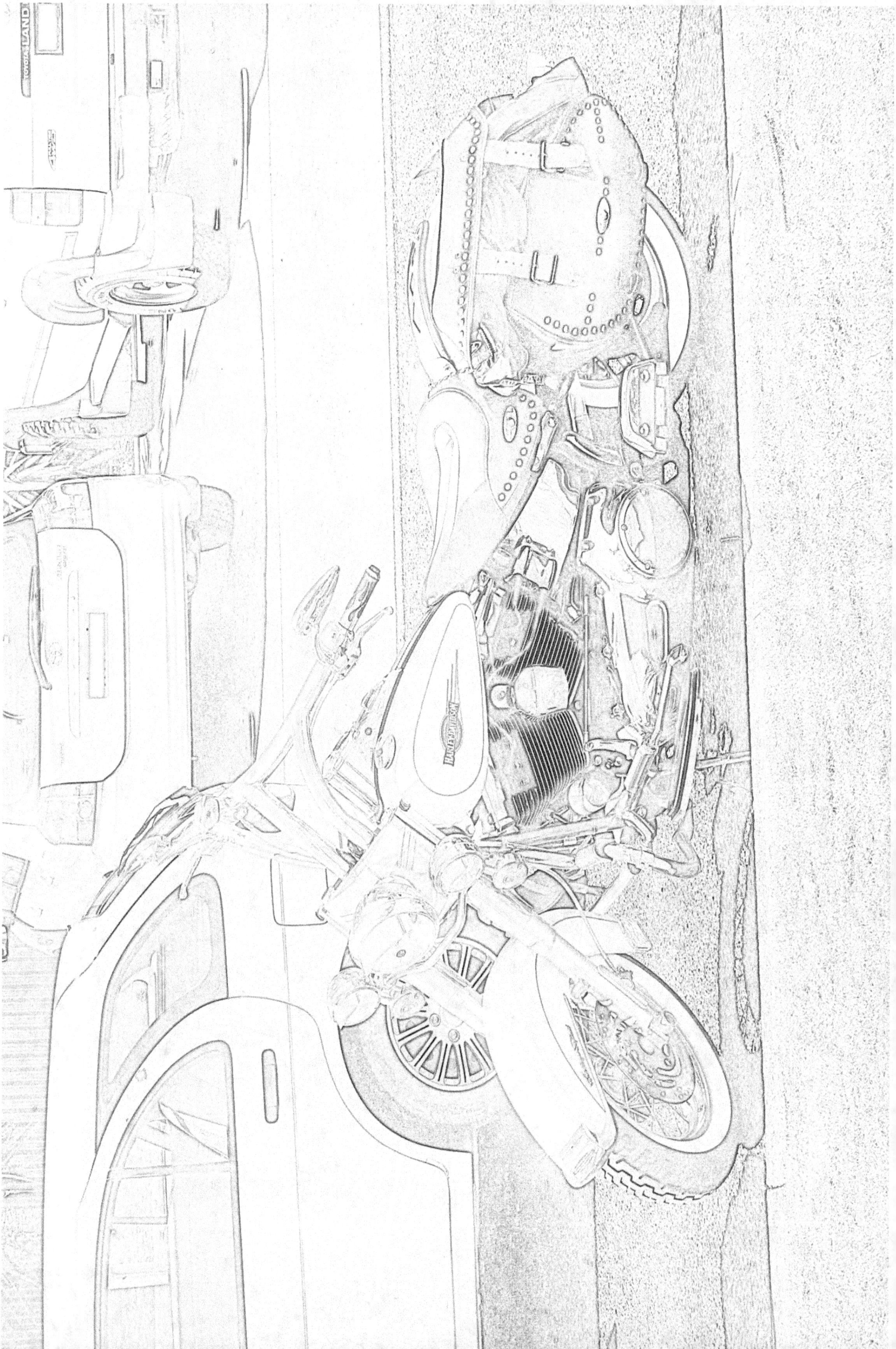
HARLEY-DAVIDSON

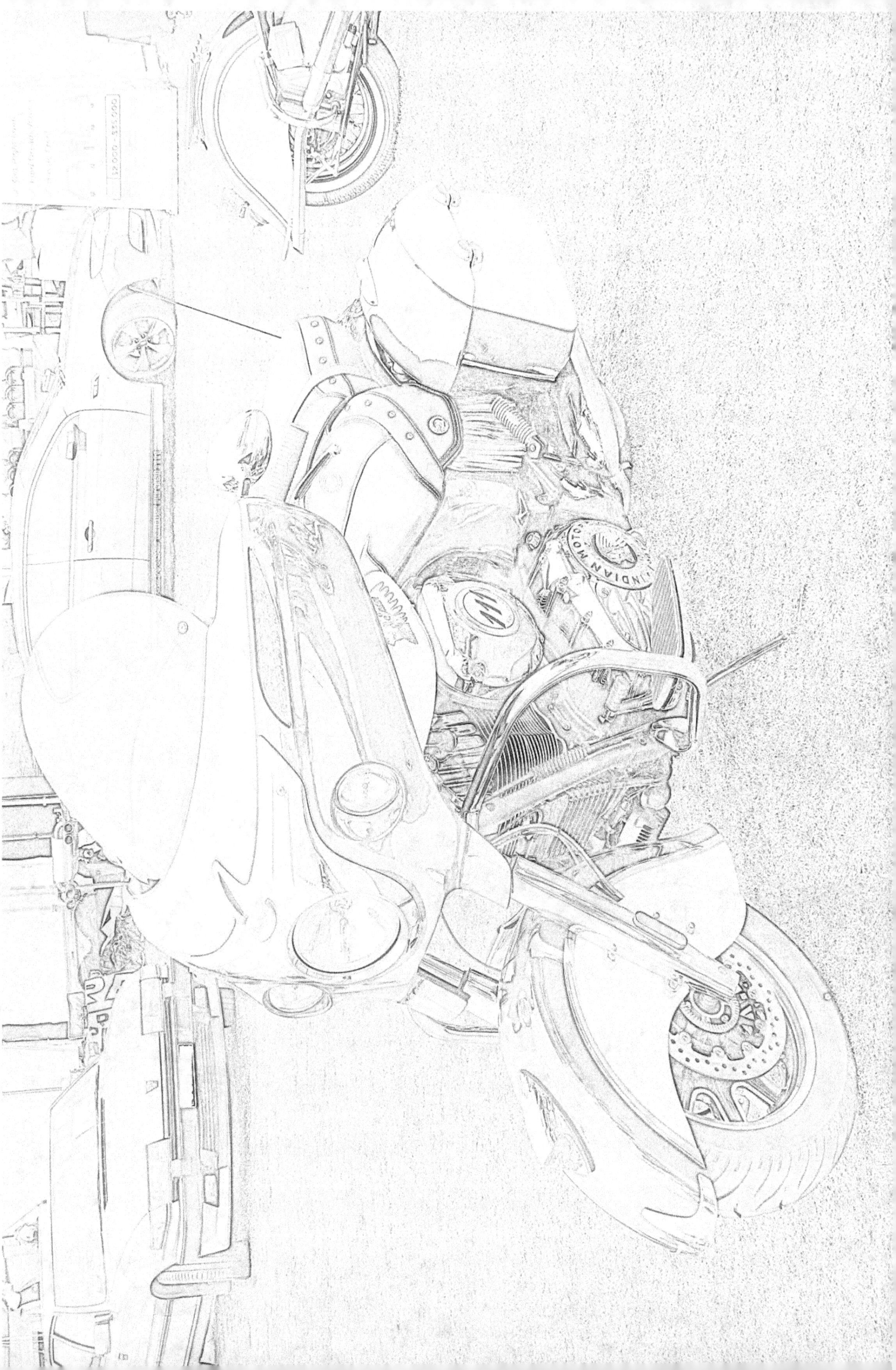

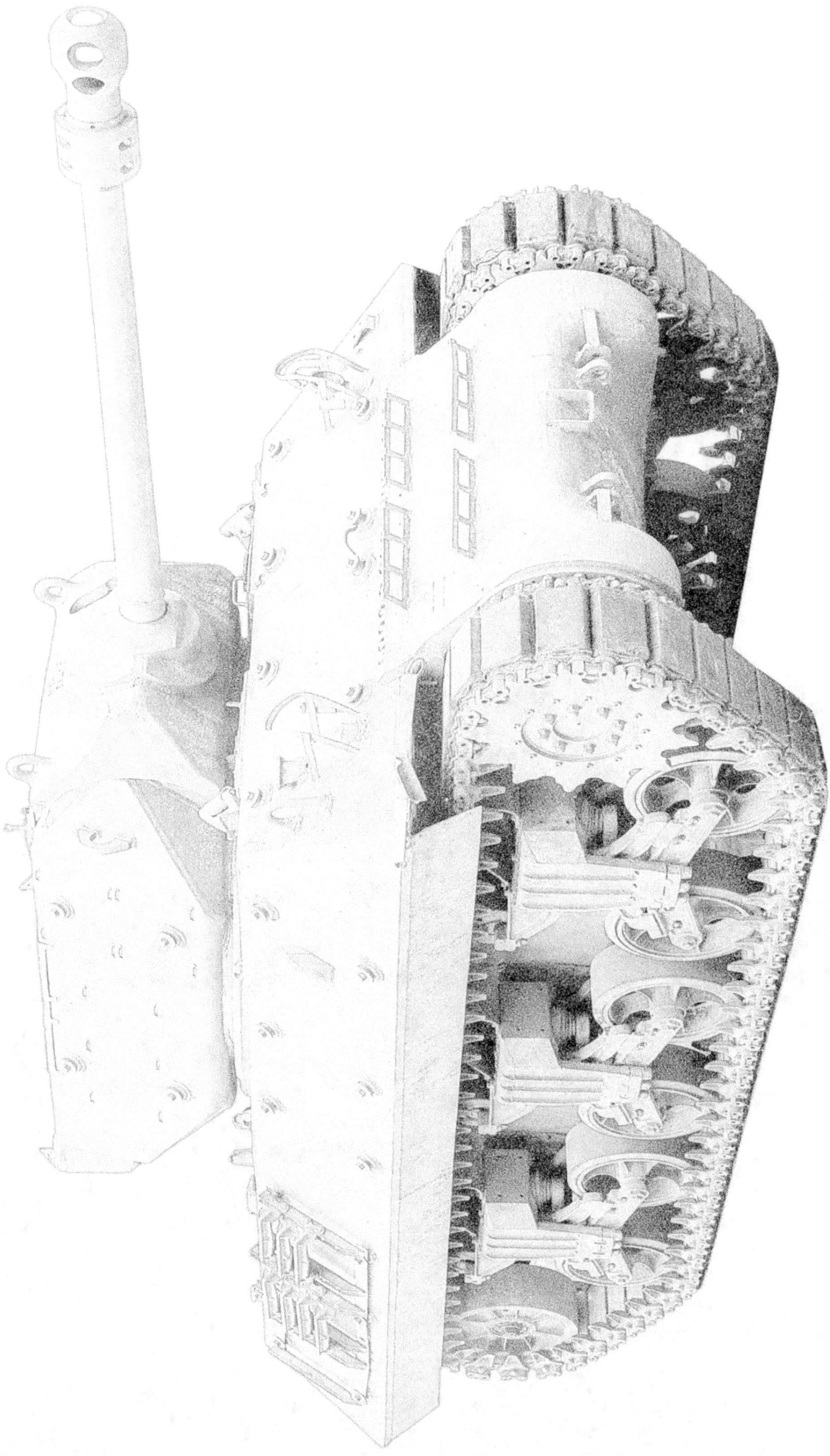

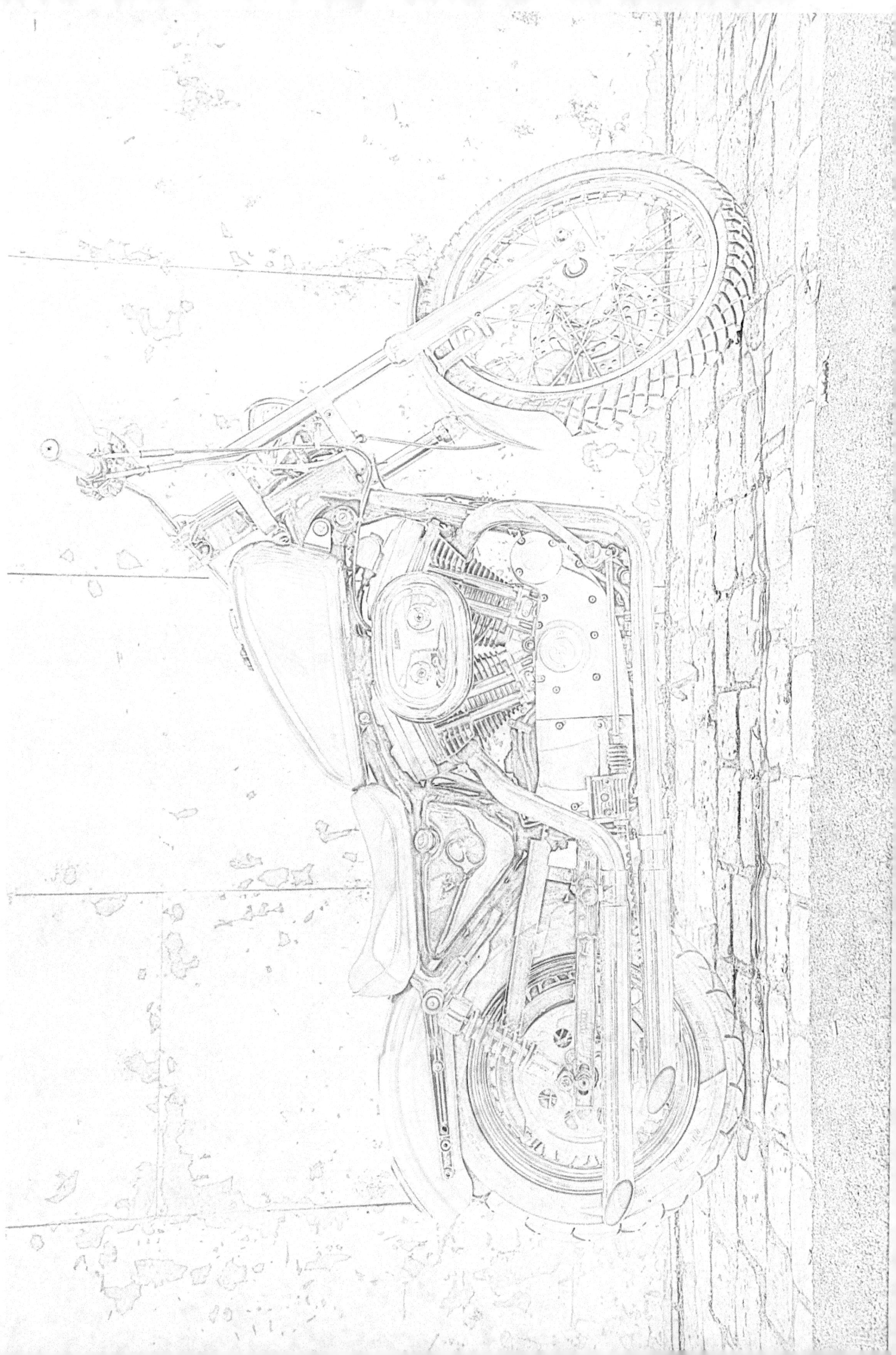

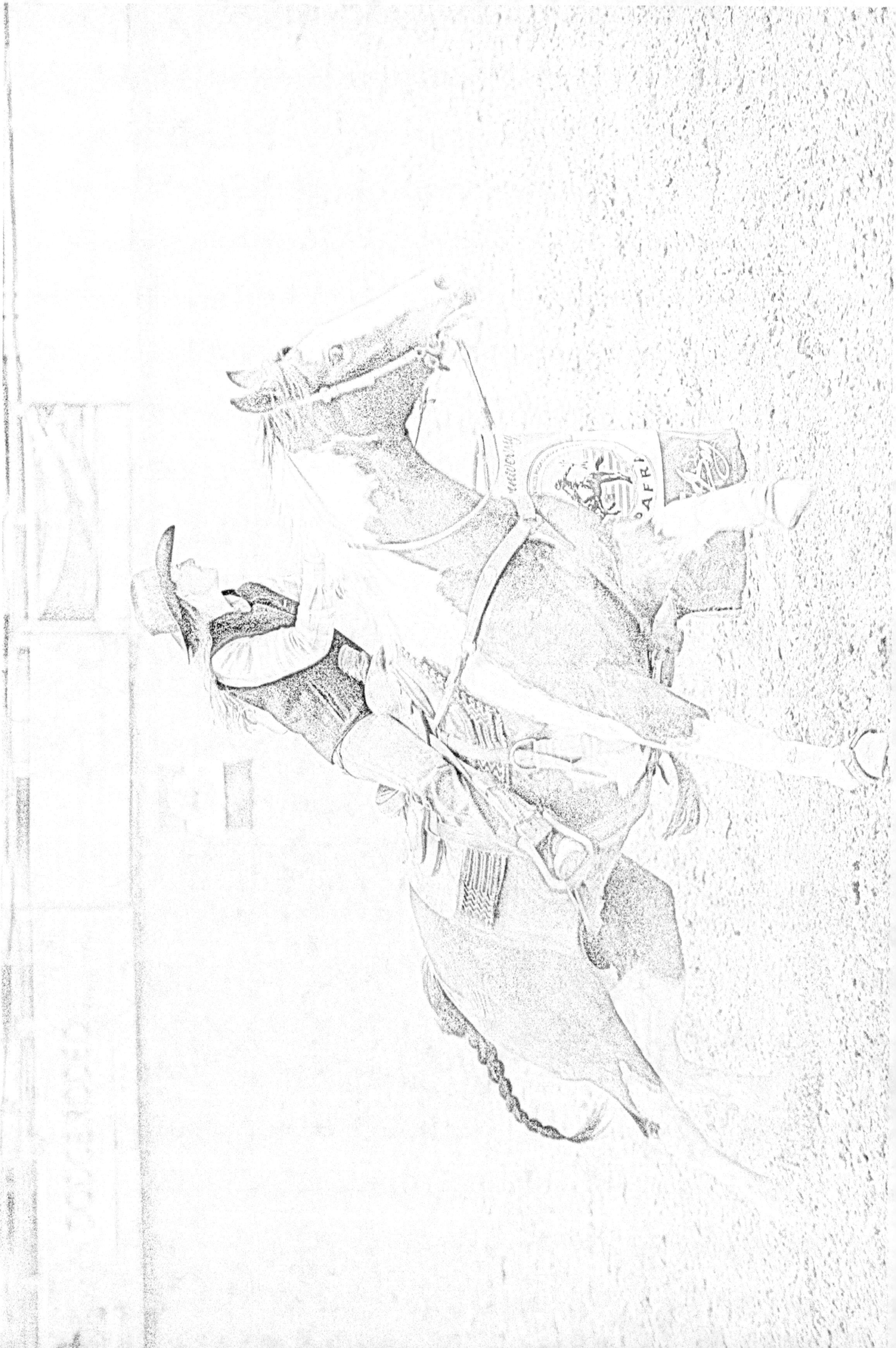

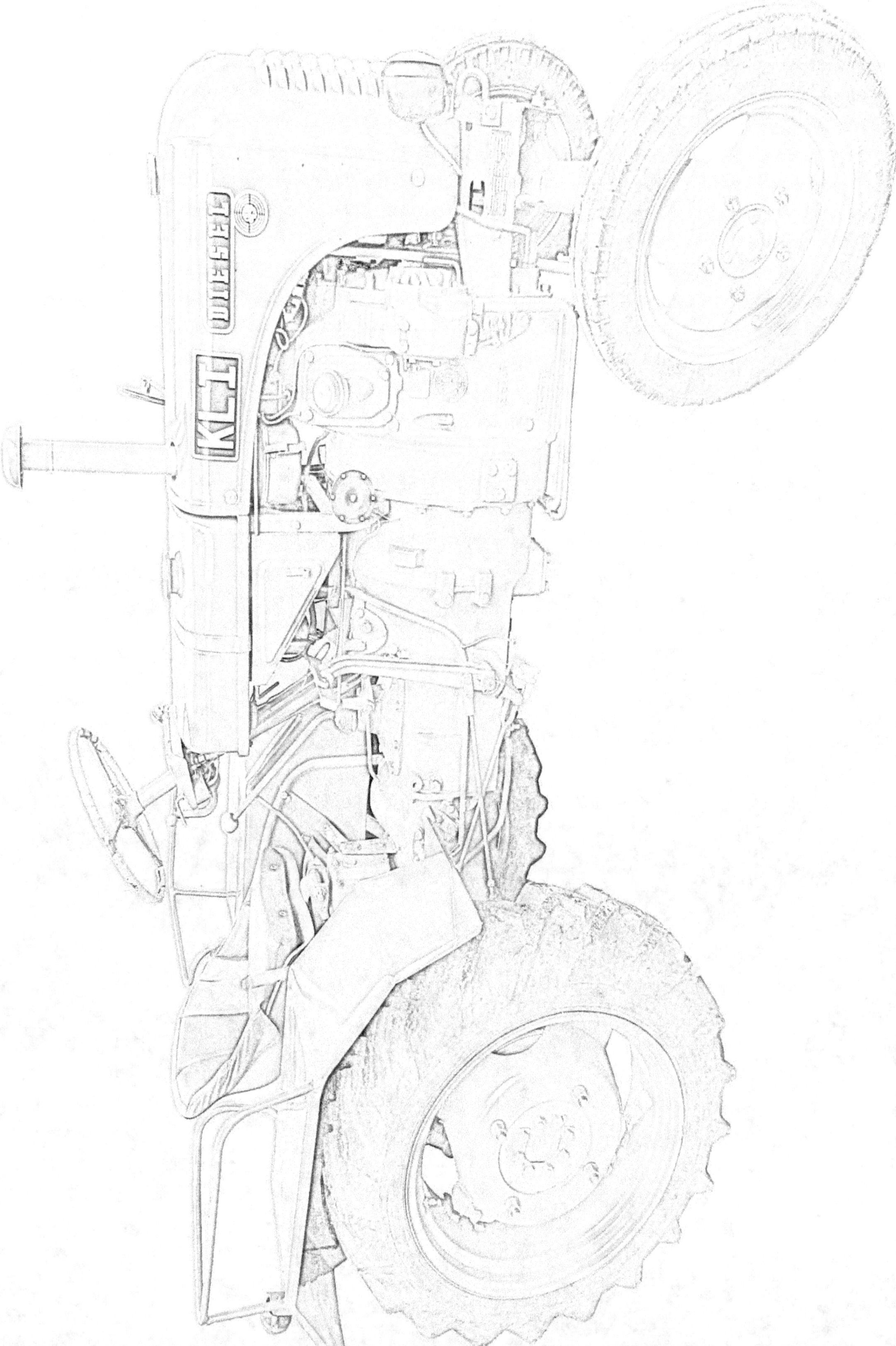

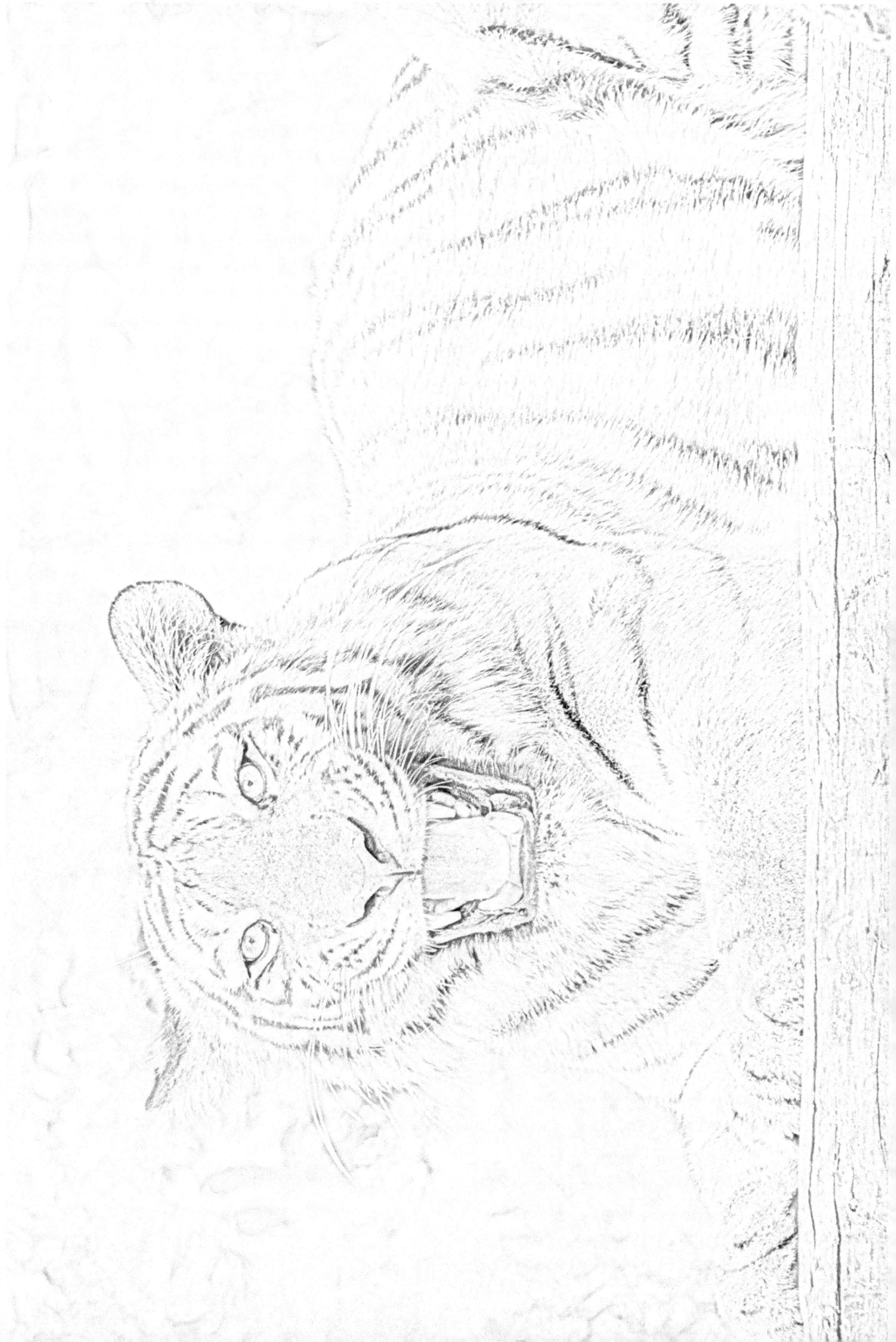

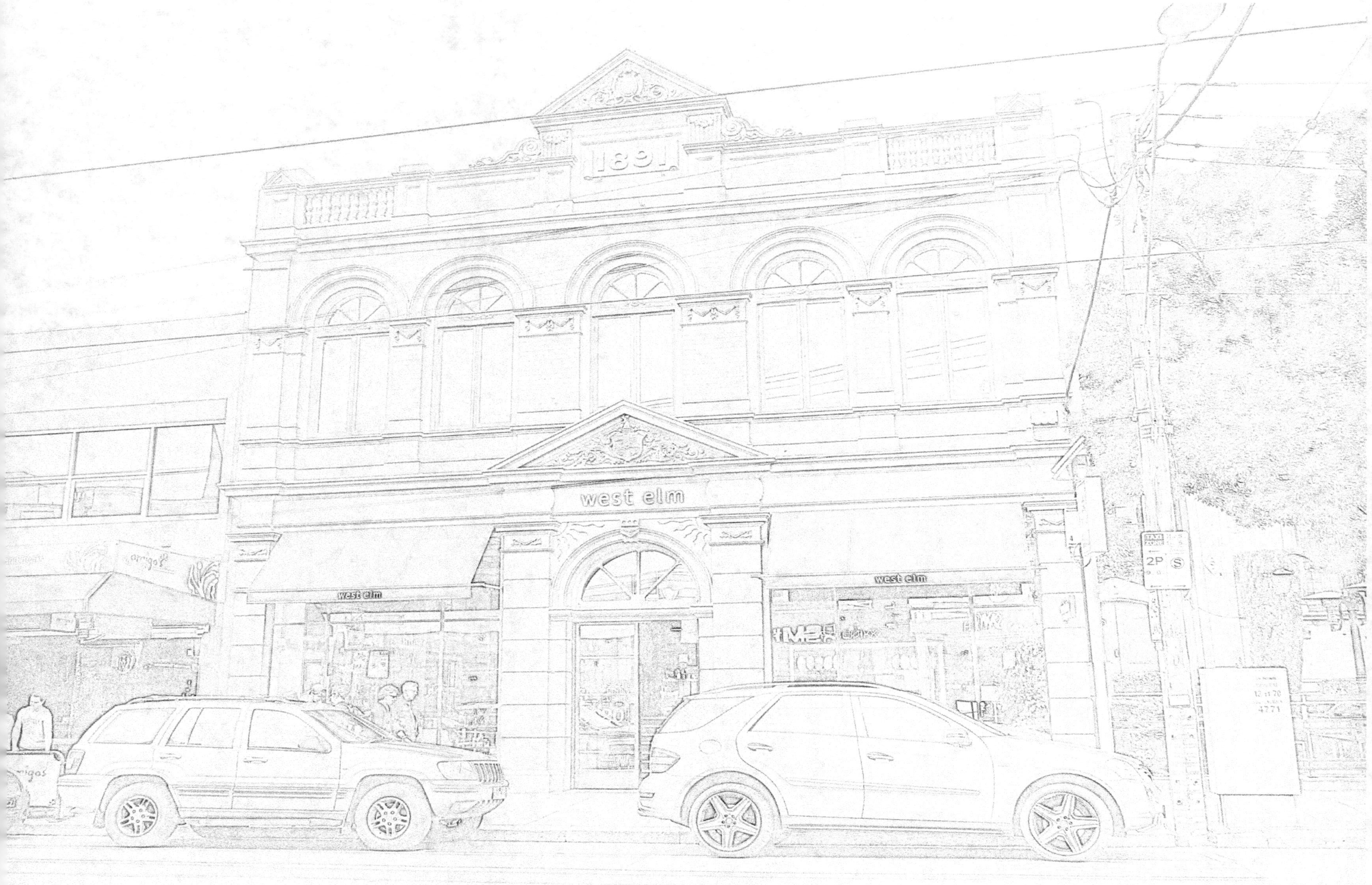
1891
west elm
west elm
west elm
2P

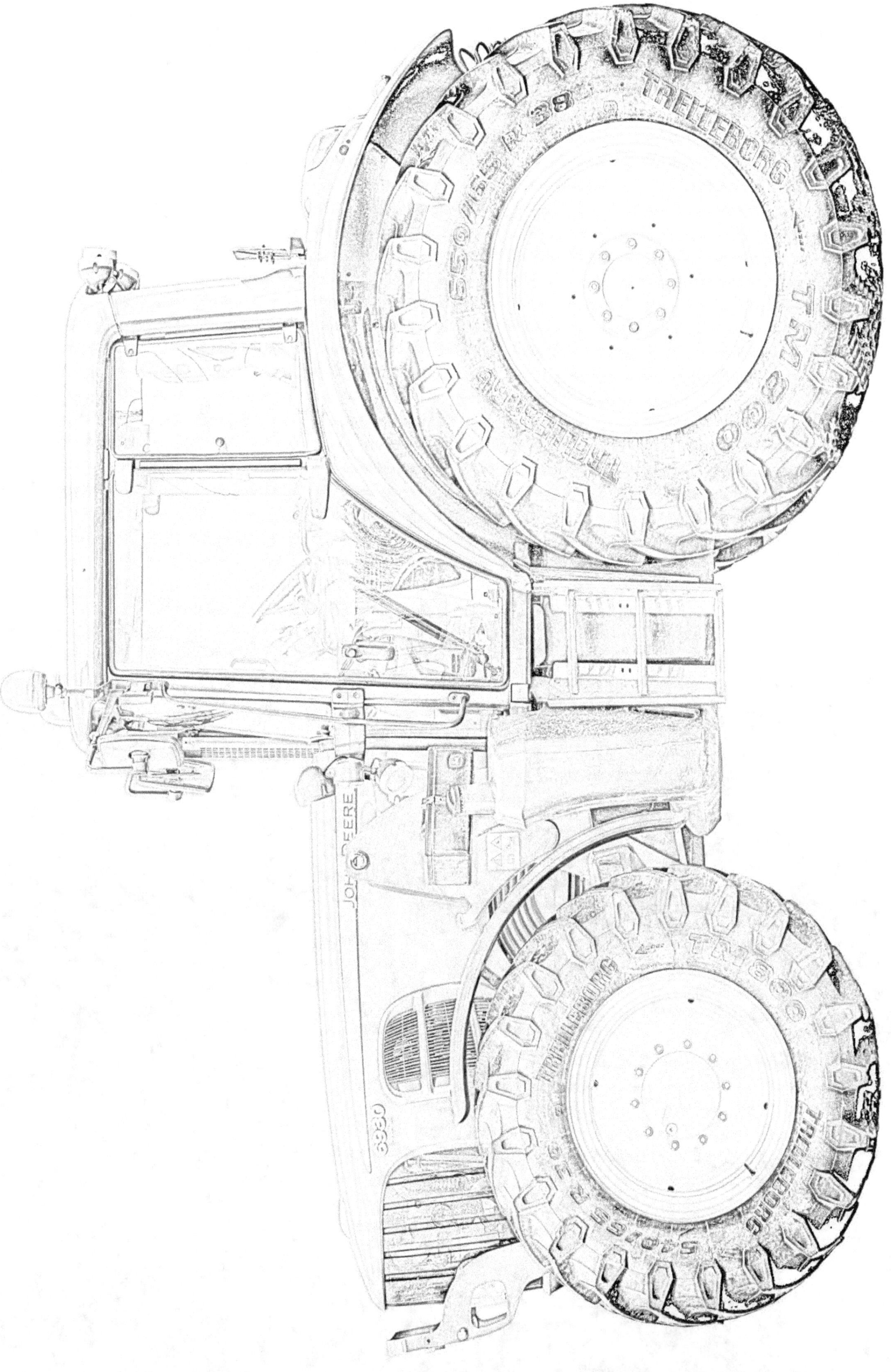
TRELLEBORG
TM800

INDIAN RIVER
TRANSPORT
INDIAN RIVER
TRANSPORT
DD155372
1046
TEXAS

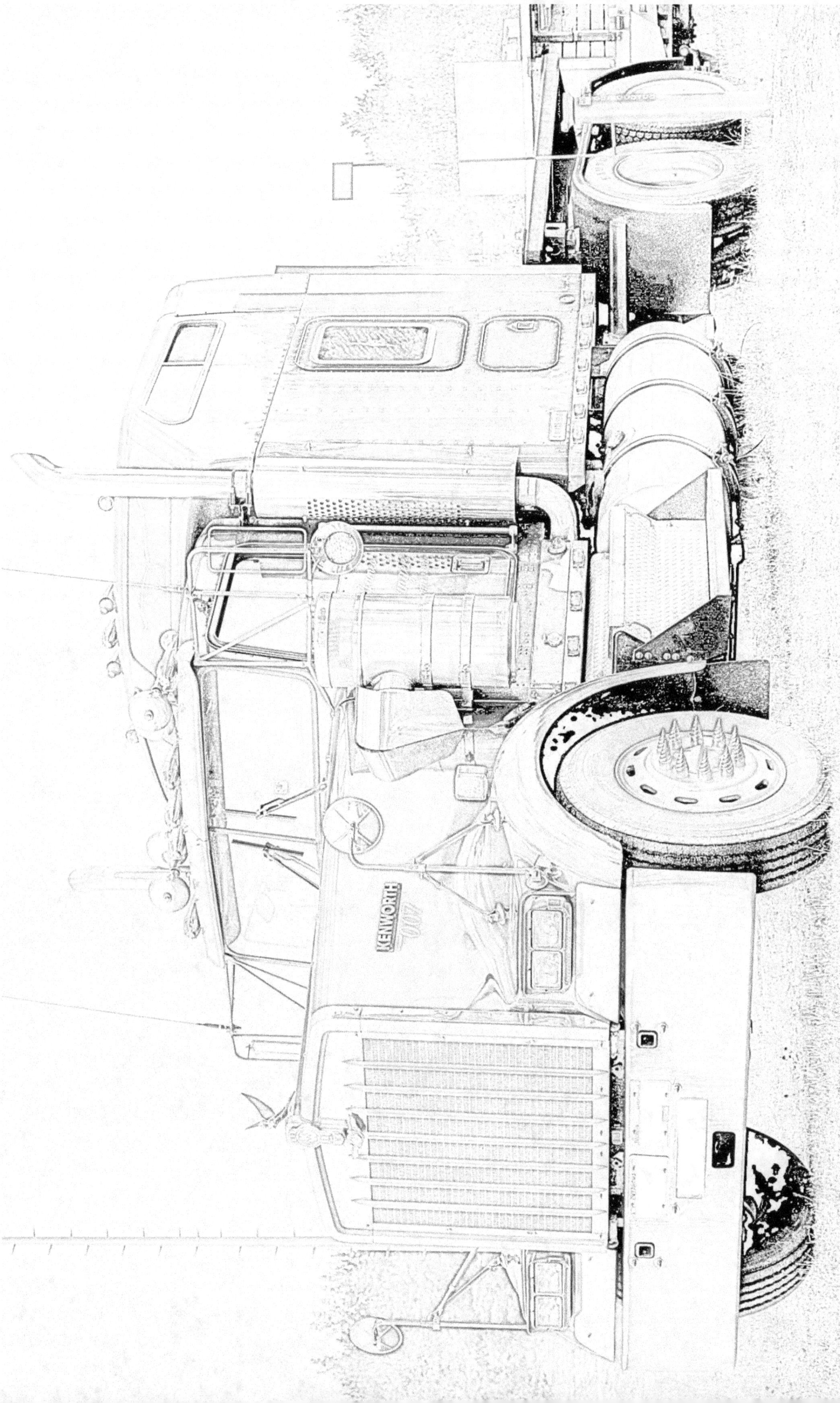
KENWORTH

www.ingramcontent.com/pod-product-compliance
Lightning Source LLC
Chambersburg PA
CBHW081055180526
45170CB00005B/1771